Hell in the hands of a Gracious God

An exploration of faith and Hell

in light of a purposeful God

By Terry McCall

ISBN: 0-9848476-1-8
ISBN-13: 978-0-9848476-1-7

DEDICATION

I dedicate this book to my wife, Amy.
She shows me the meaning of :
"but the greatest of these is love."

Cover Design by Terry Dean McCall

Art work by

Willem van de Velde II (1633-1707)

"The Gust"

CONTENTS

1 HUGGERMUGGER

Our family's all-time favorite board game is Huggermugger. In one of the game's challenges, a team is given one minute to list 12 words using any of the letters in a word such as "illustrate". So the team goes to work scribbling down words using the letters : i-l-l-u-s-t-r-a-t-e. Words begin to appear: "at" "ate" "rate" "state" "ill" "us" "rust" and "trust"—you get the point.

We face a similar challenge in the Christian faith. We have "letters", those ancient writings, the scriptures, whose elements we arrange and rearrange as best we see fit, trying to come up with some words that can be our own. We're looking for words that can be clustered into statements that bring meaning to faith and life. These statements become the answers to questions that faith and life ask of us, questions that range from purpose to destiny.

As Christians, we read the Bible and we want to make sense of it. Written long ago, it's a book that requires interpretation, and an understanding of those times. The writers communicate in parables, and we need to discover their meaning. These messages were written for us and we want to know what we are being told.

For thousands of years believers, as individuals and as community, have been issuing statements that they believe represent the faith—a faith handed down to them and a faith they must now hand down to others. These statements are as varied as the generations and the cultures that have issued them. These statements are as numerous as the denominations, sub-denominations, sects and independent groups that make up the church, a number some would say is in the hundreds.

As believers we rally under the cross, but we vary in our understanding of the cross. We rally under the cross because we believe the cross makes a difference in the world yet we simultaneously draw our lines in the sand at the foot of the cross. We love the cross but we also love our distinctive. Some lines drawn are purely to differentiate. Other lines become a cry to battle.

In this book I explore options regarding faith and Hell in light of the cross. Traditional Christianity has compiled statements and passed them down to all of us. Many in the church are content to adopt the statements handed down to them and they, with the church over them, will hand the same statements down to the next generation.

Traditions, whether we seek them or not, add to the complexity of the church. When we worship, where we worship, how we worship, all become ordered by past precedence. What we believe and how we behave as believers is also ordered and organized and handed down to the faithful.

The non-traditionalists have always been among us. Some are skeptics by nature while some just need to process things themselves before they own them. Many have felt compelled to scrutinize the statements handed down. The risk has always been that the scrutiny is viewed as mutiny. Mutiny, however, does not always have a bad ending.

This scrutiny, even if it is mutinous in nature, is not a call to abandon ship, or even a call to abandon statements. It is only a call to consider alternatives. I consider alternatives because I sense some of the statements handed down are at odds with the faith I have come to embrace.

Alternatives, whether we seek them or not, make up the theology of the church. Take Christology, the study of Jesus Christ. There are varying positions about Christ's relation to the godhead, about the virgin birth, regarding the union of his divine nature with his human nature and about his impeccability. There are also varying positions about Jesus' relationship to the human race, about his humiliation, atonement and death, his descent into Hell, his ascent into

Heaven, his current ministry, his second coming, his role in judgment and his place in glory.

And these are just a few of the areas within Christology about which there are a variety of views. Bible students and scholars apply the interpretive process to more than a dozen other "...ologies" that make up Christian doctrine, such as :

Bibliology (the study of the Scriptures),

Anthropology (the study of man),

Theology Proper (the study of God),

Hamartiology (the study of sin),

Soteriology (the study of salvation),

Ecclesiology (the study of the church),

Pneumatology (the study of the Holy Spirit),

Eschatology (the study of things to come).

Within each of these there are as many alternatives, as many lines drawn in the sand, as with Christology. An easy approach to the myriad differences is to conclude that everyone else is wrong and that we alone are right—an awkward place to be if you have an ounce of humility.

The human mind will always take the data we perceive and attempt to make sense of it. We will break things down, separate things out, categorize if we have the categories, analyze to the extent that we can analyze, and then conclude as best we can. It seems that until final clarity comes, the scriptures will be subject to such processes.

It is a good thing for humans to engage in these interpretive processes. For most who have done so, it is primarily a genuine quest to know better the God who has spoken and an equally genuine quest to understand His will for their lives. Their puzzling, and their arranging and rearranging of the pieces is an attempt to end up with a picture that helps them visualize what this spiritual dimension of life is all about and what that means for their crowded life in the subway and their tranquil time in the garden. What does it mean in the office cubicle and on the factory floor? What do these statements mean as we gather around the table and tuck our children in at night?

Many pictures have emerged from humans' quest to know God, yet we find familiar features common to most. At the center is a God who is eternal and loving and benevolent toward all. Most pictures reveal a fallen world very much in need of regeneration and redemption. And most feature common themes of faith and duty and hope and afterlife.

This book participates in that ongoing quest for a clearer picture—more puzzling, more arranging and rearranging of the pieces. It is not an attempt to create a different picture for the sake of being different, but rather an attempt to find harmony between the pieces, which, admittedly, most others do as well.

One of the early learning activities many of us encountered as toddlers was the task of passing four differently shaped pieces of wood through the corresponding holes in a wooden board. We learned that square shapes pass best through square holes and round shapes pass best through round holes. We came to understand that correspondence can be a helpful friend as we navigate this world around us.

I have concluded that it is fair for me to expect correspondence when it comes to things of faith. It seems reasonable to me that the God who has ordered this universe with all its corresponding elements has ordered the spiritual dimension in the same way. The plan of God will correspond with his nature. The purpose of humanity will correspond with God's plan.

If we believe that God is by nature an awesome God who is holy, loving, gracious, merciful and kind, then we would expect his purpose for us to be shaped by that same nature. A rather commonly accepted statement regarding our purpose in relation to this awesome God is that we are created and placed here on planet earth to know God and enjoy him forever. That statement touches both our purpose and our destiny. That statement corresponds with the nature of God as I have come to understand it, and therefore shapes my expectation of every Christian teaching.

One aspect of Christian teaching that lacks this correspondence for me is that related to Hell. In my mind Hell, as taught by the traditional church, lacks correspondence. It is at odds with the very nature of things; it is at odds with the very nature of God.

Two and half decades ago, just a couple of hours before our second son was born, we knew something wasn't right. Two days later, after an attempt to preserve a life that was only meant to pass this way briefly, the Lord gave me a verse from Deuteronomy in which Moses concluded at the end of his days that God:

> "... *is the Rock, his works are perfect,*
> *and all his ways are just.*
> *A faithful God who does no wrong,*
> *upright and just is he.*"
> *Deut. 32:4*

That verse, and the truth it speaks, informs every statement I make regarding the faith handed down to me, and that I will be handing down to others. As I consider the words I will use, in the end there must be correspondence between those statements and the goodness and justice of God.

I recently fleshed out in writing Hell as taught by traditional Christianity. I gave it substance. I treated Hell as destiny and not just doctrine. I imagined it in time. I imagined it from the church's position that it is eternal. I fleshed it out from the perspective that apart from Christ there is no salvation (a view I believe), that apart from Christ ones goes to Hell (another view I believe), and from the perspective that Hell is never ending (a view I question).

I fleshed out the concept of Hell based on the story of Billy. Billy was fourteen when he lost control of his bicycle and was hit by a car and died. Billy had been to a church meeting two months earlier in which the Gospel was preached and an invitation was made for any and all to accept Jesus as Savior. Mrs. Wellington, Billy's Sunday school teacher, was praying for Billy. She was praying and peeking through a thinly slit eye, hoping for movement, knowing that Billy understood the issues. Billy did not move. Actually, during most of the meeting Billy was thinking about a new bike he had seen at the local hardware store. During the invitation to accept Jesus, Billy was thinking about when he could best exit his pew so as to arrive at the church door about the same time as his classmate Cindy, with whom he wanted to talk about the new bike he was considering.

Billy's funeral was a sad occasion. Death brings grief. Words of encouragement were offered and the Christian hope was set before all. But Mrs. Wellington went home heartsick because, despite the hope we have in Christ, Billy had not availed himself of that hope and was now hopelessly lost. Mrs. Wellington dutifully passed the current information through the filters of the church's traditions about the life and faith and afterlife and had no choice but to conclude that Billy died and went to Hell, that place of torment, that place where he is eternally separated from his Maker.

If we believe in Hell, we must be willing to flesh out Hell. And if our understanding of Hell speaks in terms of eternity as the traditional church does, we must be willing to fast forward in our fleshing. We must be willing to project forward a billion years and see Billy trapped in a world of torment, still weeping as when he entered, still gnashing teeth, still contending with the worm that never dies. We must be willing to take the billion years times 365 and number the days. We must be willing to take the days times twenty-four and number the hours. We must be willing to take the hours times sixty and number the minutes. We must be willing to take a minute of our day, even this minute, and imagine such separation, such lost-ness, such sadness, such torment. Are you slowly counting to sixty?

We must then be willing to fast forward a trillion years, and a gazillion years, and realize that even that far out it is only the beginning of eternity. It becomes a sobering picture.

That scenario, which is in keeping with the church's view of Hell, does not harmonize with the picture that emerges as I read the Bible. My experience has been that few in the church are comfortable with this picture. They have no problem with the likes of Adolf Hitler going off to such torment, but surely not Billy, surely not as this author has just fleshed things out.

I have no desire to remove Hell from the equation. I believe in Hell. I believe Hell is an afterlife experience. I believe that I am safe in telling one and all, "You don't want to die and go to Hell." I believe it is a place of torment, a place of weeping, a place of teeth gnashing, a place of separation.

I also believe in a sovereign God, a just God, a God who hates sin and who judges sin. I believe in a holy God who has an eternal detestation for sin. I believe that we are saved by grace through faith. I believe no one comes to the Father except through Jesus Christ. And as already stated, I believe in a literal, afterlife Hell. I do, however, feel compelled to look anew at the letters and see if other words can be formed, if another arrangement is possible.

I work with the same letters as other evangelical conservative Christians. I no doubt define some things differently, which allows for arrangements that are otherwise difficult. This book is about my arrangement. It is not meant to be a doctrinal statement, but rather one believer's attempt to arrange the letters in a way that allows for statements that makes sense to him. This book is about exploring interpretive possibilities that seem more in keeping with my understanding of God and his purposes.

2 A PUSH AWAY

My wife and I and our three children had recently returned from Kenya where we had served as missionaries for seven years. We were staying with my parents, catching up with family, and considering the options for the next chapter of our life.

It was a bright, sunny mid-morning in July. I had been at my laptop for several hours, corresponding via e-mail, when my body and spirit said, "Enough, time to get up and move a bit." I pushed away from the table and went outside. My folks still lived in the house where they raised my four siblings and me. A lot of memories reside on those three acres. We lived in rural western Pennsylvania, where neighbors were a good shout away and the woods was our playground. I loved climbing trees as a kid. It was one form of self-elevation that no one looked down on.

Standing in the sunshine, having pushed away from my laptop, looking out over the landscape of my youth, my body hoping for something other than sediment, I wanted to climb. I considered a dozen trees that all had inviting limbs reaching out in all directions as if to say, "Whosoever will, let him come." I looked at the side of my Dad's garage. It had steel siding, it was ten foot to the square, and it had nothing that lent itself to being climbed. Then I had one of those moments in which my right hand comes up and I grasp my chin between my thumb and forefinger, that universal sign that some thinking was taking place. In less than a minute I saw it all quite clearly. If I was to make a round disc, say eight feet in diameter, and put a hub at the center and mount it to the wall and put some climbing holds on the surface, this disc would rotate and you could climb endlessly.

My brother John lives down the road from my parents. John is one of those people who make it very easy to ask: "Hey, could you give a guy a hand?" because the response is always the same: "Sure!" So I called John to see if he was free. Four minutes later he arrived driving his pickup. I explained my idea to him and off we went to the lumber yard for some plywood, and then to a junk yard to pull a hub from an old car. Before the sun set, we had an ugly prototype of my invention hanging on the back wall of Dad's garage. We had nailed some blocks of wood on the surface to act as climbing holds, and then we had the nieces and nephews climb on to give it a try. They were our test pilots. Sure enough, there seemed to be something to the idea.

That day was almost ten years ago. That idea of a rotating climbing wall evolved, became patented, and today my sons and I are building "Freedom Climbers." We have seen them featured on TV shows like Extreme Makeover: Home Edition, Man Cave, and the Gadget Show in the UK. We have installations in fourteen countries and in facilities ranging from military bases to YMCAs, from private residences to apartment complex fitness rooms, from corporate offices to schools and universities. But this book is not about the Freedom Climber. It is about the possibilities that exist when we push away from the table and explore options, when our body and spirit say, "I need something else here."

When I chaired the Bible Department at Rift Valley Academy in Kijabe, Kenya, I taught juniors and seniors a course in Christian doctrine. Rift Valley Academy is a boarding school for the children of missionaries who come from a tremendously rich variety of backgrounds. We had kids whose parents were missionaries with Baptist organizations from the southern U.S states. Some students were children of parents sent out by Pentecostal churches in Denmark. We taught kids whose families were fundamentalists from New England, kids whose upbringing was in a Presbyterian environment in South Korea, kids from liberal traditions, kids from conservative traditions. There were Calvinists and there were Wesleyans. There were millennialists and amillennialists. There were pacifists and activists. My task was to respect the various traditions from which they came, to expose the students to various basic positions in Christian doctrine, and ultimately to point them toward a means of identifying doctrines that would underpin their efforts to honor and follow Christ and to fulfill their calling in life.

One of the exercises I gave my students at the end of the course in doctrine was to look at the body of information and answer the question, "For which of the doctrines that we have studied would you go to the stake?" In other words, for which of these Christian teachings were they willing to lay down their life? Suddenly, topics that generated considerable discussion in the classroom were crossed off and the list began to shrink.

I noticed something interesting as I was teaching doctrine. When we were looking at theology proper and discussing the attributes and nature of God, the students for the most part absorbed the information. Regardless of their tradition, they seemed to reach consensus that these propositional statements about what we should attribute to God were universally accepted as true. And the reason for this is that the church has historically ascribed to God only what he has revealed about himself. No student objected to the claims that God is Almighty, everywhere present, all knowing, compassionate, loving, merciful, long suffering and so on. The objections in the class room came when we started sorting through things like predestination, or the interpretation of future things, or the gifts of the Spirit, or the governmental structure of the church and a woman's place within those structures.

That observation led me to conclude that the nature and attributes of God trump questionable doctrines. The attributes are God revealed. The debatable, questionable, sometimes controversial doctrines are, on the other hand, our attempt to make sense of scripture. It seems that if these were clear, like the attributes, there would be no controversy.

I am writing these pages at a moment when there is much debate about Hell. It is not a new debate, but it is vigorous. A decade ago I pushed away from a table, weary from e-mails. I went outside to consider options for my body and spirit. For the last couple of decades of my Christian journey, I have been considering options when it comes to the letters and words that shape our understanding of Hell. I have pushed away from the table, stepped outside, and have considered options that are, to my mind, feasible. These are not something for which I would go to the stake, but then again, neither is the traditional view of Hell something for which I would die.

I have inhabited the evangelical and conservative circles of the Christian faith here in the United States and abroad since the mid-1970s. Most in those circles would take exception to questioning the traditional view of Hell. The interesting thing is, in the several thousand sermons I have heard through the years, there may have been a dozen sermons about Hell. For the most part, Hell was only a tiny and rare blip on the radar.

Hell, for most churches, is like a light green leisure suit we keep in our church basement. We almost seem embarrassed to bring it up, and when we do it just doesn't seem a good fit. It just doesn't correspond with the nature of things; it seems out of place.

Yet Hell is part of the judgment of God. God's judgments are good. I believe Hell should not be an embarrassment for the church, and I believe it can be a good fit. Hell deserves more attention in the Church than it gets. I believe Hell should occupy the same space on our landscape as it did on the landscape of Christ's ministry.

I have a high view of the ministry and work of Christ. I have a high view of the judgment of God. This book is about glorifying God and raising Hell. But we begin in the garden.

3 ADAM AND US, WE HEAR VOICES

Twenty-some years ago I owned a Ford Escort with a manual transmission. I had returned home from running errands, pulled up the driveway, had gotten out and entered the house. Just as the screened door closed behind me, I heard a crash across the street. I stepped back out on the porch to see what had happened. I saw that a red Escort, just like mine, was halfway up on the porch of the house across the street, the driver apparently having fled. Then I noticed that my driveway was empty and realized the Escort was mine. The impact bent the car's frame, not to mention the damage it did to the neighbor's porch. Someone had left the Escort in neutral and had failed to set the brake. Since I had driven it last, everyone tended to point their finger at me. I was never convinced it was completely my fault, it seemed to me that gravity had some culpability as well. The Escort was drivable and the body shop was nearby. The bent frame left the car pulling to the left in a sinister kind of way ("sinister" being Latin for 'left-handed').

I mention this story because I think that Adam was originally like a car in neutral. The plan was: listen to the Maker, respond accordingly, and Adam would find himself freely moving gently down a slope through the blessings of God, frame intact, neighbors glad he was part of the neighborhood. The Maker had said, in essence, "Enjoy the garden, just mind that one tree in the middle."

> *"You are free to eat from any tree in the garden; but you must not*
> *eat from the tree of the knowledge of good and evil,*
> *for when you eat of it you will surely die."*
> *Gen. 2:16,17*

It seems to me that to understand the human predicament, we have to understand Adam and his decisions. I was back home recently in the place I grew up, and back among some of the old prejudices that will only die out as one generation gives way to another, if even then. It dawned on me that the voices we heed shape our lives.

As the garden scene unfolds, there were four voices:

God speaking instructionally: "You are free to eat... but..."

Adam speaking creatively: "I think I'll call this a 'dog.'"

Eve speaking collaboratively: "Let's go with 'canus domesticates.'"

The serpent speaking doubtfully: "Did God really say, 'you must not eat ...?'" The serpent speaking even deceitfully: "You will not surely die ..."

If we ask why God would allow the voice of doubt in the midst of paradise, perhaps it has something to do with paradise being the realm where his relationship with humanity was to be played out. At the heart of any true love relationship there must be trust. Love that has a history of faithfulness embedded in it, a faithfulness that is a contribution of all parties, that love is the strongest, most enduring love attainable. That love always protects, always trusts, always hopes, always perseveres. That love never fails.

Certain churches have a series of questions they put to their young members, and a series of corresponding answers. They are called catechisms. It is indoctrination. It is not a bad thing. Catechism teaches the youth of the church the church's answers to faith and life questions. One question that arises, and one we should all be working through is the question, "What is the chief end of man?" In other words, "Why have we been created?" and "What will be our ultimate end?"

I find many people, including myself, quite comfortable with the answer given in a document called the Westminster Shorter Catechism. Its response to the question, "What is the chief end of man?" is the following:

"Man's chief end is to glorify God and enjoy him forever."

Adam and Eve were placed in the garden to glorify God and enjoy him forever. Adam and Eve were placed in an environment where God would use time to demonstrate His love and faithfulness in this relationship. Equipped with all they needed for life and godliness, Adam and Eve were also given time and opportunity to love God faithfully.

We glorify God as our opinion of God is shaped by our experiences with God, and we express that opinion in testimony and song. The Greek word for 'glory' is "doxa," from which we get Doxology. The Doxology is that short song that goes:

"Praise God from whom all blessing flow, Praise him all creatures here below."

As is often the case, the root of the word helps in our understanding of the meaning. Doxa, at a root level, means "opinion"—not the opinion that crops up on talk shows and among talking heads and bloggers that fill the airways, but rather an opinion that is grounded in something permanent. If I tell you it is my opinion that "God is gracious and patient and loving and almighty, and that He wants me to hate what is evil and cling to what is good," then, because that opinion is rooted in something permanent, the eternal word of God, there is glory connected to that opinion. I have glorified God with that opinion. Every time we share a good testimony that reinforces a truth about God, that testimony brings glory to God.

In the garden, the Doxology should have been ever flowing from the lips of this son and daughter of God. The garden should have been filled with "Praise God from whom all blessing flow." This was their chief end.

Adam and Eve were created and placed in the Garden that they might experience the blessings of God and acknowledge those blessings before their Maker and one another. God, in time and space, proves himself faithful. Our opinion is shaped by the blessings that flow and the faithfulness that is demonstrated. Our opinion is shaped as he keeps his promises to a thousand generations. His glory is declared as we share these convictions, these opinions, with a thousand generations. Adam and Eve were to glorify God and enjoy Him forever. Theirs was to be a relationship built on the faithful acknowledgment of the blessings that flowed.

Enter the voice of doubt.

Adam and Eve had great latitude to explore self-actualization, to achieve their potential. It was the voice of doubt that suggested exploring self-determination, a suggestion of the adversary and not the Advisor. Happy is the person who allows God to determine what life is meant to be, and then finds the freedom in Him to explore all the potentialities. But happiness was slipping into the shadows for Adam and Eve as the prospects of self-determination yielded visions of Godlikeness.

"For God knows that when you eat of it your eyes will be opened, and you will be like God..."
Gen. 3:5

Adam felt a tug and his orientation was slightly altered, another tug and he was being turned, another tug and his back was facing the light and he was in the shadow of his own rebellion. This orientation gave the new voice preeminence. This voice became the new voice of promise, ensuring an existence that went beyond sustenance; it included a change of status, a becoming like God. Adam bit and the rest is history.

There was indeed a change of status as we all know. The security of the garden was lost, the blessings more remote, the frame was bent, and the neighbor's porch was damaged. Adam had failed to apply the brake.

When I think about our fallen state and our alienation from God, I tend to see it as a choice we made to allow other voices to dominate the landscape of the human experience. God's original intent was that we be moved along by One True Voice. We chose otherwise. We have chosen lesser voices. We now live in a conflicted state. Correspondence is difficult, as many voices are vying for supremacy. At one moment we find ourselves paralyzed, immobile, surrounded by competing voices. Then in the next moment we find ourselves racing down a slope in mob fashion toward treacherous waters, responding to a call but not even sure who the caller is.

Those are the extremes. There are also the thousand moments between, in which we snap out of a thought process and ask ourselves, "Where did that come from?" We lay restless in bed. We give poor counsel based on poor voices. We make bad choices based on bad voices. Our impure motives are grounded in impure voices. We reluctantly agree with Pink Floyd that "There's someone in my head but it's not me."

Certainly there are good voices around us. And certainly we ourselves are called to be good voices. There are times I celebrate the variety of voices in the world. At other times I long for one voice: one single, trustworthy voice giving meaning to life, determining life, shaping life as it was originally intended to be, and inviting me to explore the potentialities of life within its framework.

Disobedience, at its most basic level, is heeding voices that oppose the One True Voice. It is a dis-hearing or "refusing to hear." It is moving away from potentialities and moving more toward fatalities.

Clearly, humanity's major problem is best described as disobedience. It is disobedience to the subconscious, where God speaks those hard-to-explain 'yeas' and 'nays' that have been written on the heart. It is disobedience to the conscience that speaks of the moral expectations that our community and society have embedded in our minds. It is disobedience to the laws legislated by parents and parliament in order for our world to be a better place.

The church speaks of a fall, but I prefer to see myself as disobedient rather than fallen. I know when I am disobedient. I am not sure when I am fallen. Disobedience is the problem and obedience is the solution. When Jesus was asked which commandment was the greatest, he began his answer with the word, "Hear."

> *"Hear, O Israel, the Lord our God, the Lord is one. Love the Lord your God with all your heart and with all your soul and with all your mind and with all your strength."*
> *Matt. 22:37*

That answer, found in the New Testament, is one of the most famous passages from the Old Testament and is called in Jewish circles, the "Shema," which is the Hebrew word for "hear." Hebrew scholars tell us that both hearing and obeying are bound up in the word. When God commands us to hear, there is expectation of obedience.

Our Maker invites us to walk with him. The invitation no sooner lands on our ears than other voices ring out their offerings: "This path is more pleasurable," "This way is less demanding," "This circuit is short and familiar and always returning you to your comfort zone." Likewise, it is the opposing voices that make the second greatest commandment difficult as well.

> *"And the second is like it:*
> *'Love your neighbor as yourself.'"*
> Matt. 22:39

I consider my neighbor, think of his current challenges and I sense the voice of God suggesting actions that would move me lovingly into his space as friend and brother. But before my will initiates such actions, other voices ring out. Arguments formulate for other actions or inaction. The suggestion arises that tomorrow is a better day for involvement. And so my God's voice goes unheeded, and my neighbor's need goes unmet. And there was morning and there was evening—another day.

This fallen world in which we live is full of opposing voices that make "shema" difficult. Better voices speak, but the lesser voices speak louder. Better voices speak, but opposing voices mark the day and make the news. Better voices point toward peace and hope, while lesser voices shape our landscape with conflict and despair.

Our Maker invites us to walk with him, to know him, to hear him speak words of truth that would set us free. But in the words of a song by Daniel Lanois and made popular by Dave Matthews, we are "strangers in the eyes of the Maker." We are strangers as our lives move in directions opposing the ways of God. We are strangers as we listen to strange voices. The song, which is called "The Maker," notes our estrangement, but suggests hope. It states the problem like this:

"I could not see for the fog in my eyes,
I could not feel for the fear in my life,"

And then:

"From across the great divide, in the distance I saw a light,
John Bap'tist, walking to me with the Maker."

John the Baptist had a singular role. His task was to call people to repentance. Our estrangement from God is only resolved as we turn from the opposing voices back to the True Voice. When our orientation is one of faith, and we "work the fields of Abraham," as the song goes, the estrangement ends; for we, like Abraham, become a people of faith, a people who walk with God.

Faith and obedience put us firmly in the grasp of our Maker, who not only created us but longs to shape us as Potter. Faith and obedience make us workable clay in his hands.

Faith is an orientation that allows us to be shaped by our Maker, an orientation that puts us within hearing of the True Voice. Faith keeps our gaze God-ward and our opinion Godly. Faith brings glory to God.

I have a conviction that if humanity, in its entirety, were given to clarity, and if in that clarity we reviewed the human story and saw clearly how the opposing voices had ruined the race, how potentialities had barely been realized, how opposing voices gave rise to fatalities, we would all own the fact that we had fallen short of the glory of God.

I have a conviction that God, the Great Revealer, at the end of the day is more inclined to give clarity than to cloud, more inclined to bring people into the light than to send them off into the darkness. I believe darkness has its place. I believe Hell has its place. But I don't believe Hell should be occupying the space the traditional church has given it. If we cannot see for the fog in our eyes or the shroud that covers, it is only until the fog lifts, the shroud be removed and the separation end. Death is separation and that death will be swallowed up in victory.

"On this mountain the Lord Almighty will prepare a feast of rich food for all people, a banquet of aged wine— the best of meats and the finest of wines.

> *On this mountain he will destroy the shroud that enfolds all*
> *peoples, the sheet that covers all nations;*
> *he will swallow up death forever."*
> *Isa. 25: 6-8*

Until then we hear voices.

4 EXTREME MAKEOVER

I received an email from a member of the design team for the ABC Sunday evening TV show Extreme Makeover: Home Edition. They had become aware of my invention, the Freedom Climber, and thought it would be a good addition to a home they were building. We chatted on the phone a few times, they explained the process and we worked through the logistics. I happened to have one in inventory, so I shipped it to Idaho and thirteen days later my wife, Amy, and I were in Pocatello working shoulder to shoulder with hundreds of volunteers on the busiest construction site I had ever seen.

As is often the case with Extreme Makeover: Home Edition, this too was a heartwarming story. A family's house had been significantly damaged by fire. The family had been living in makeshift housing. The mother was a single parent, battling cancer, and raising six children. Ty Pennington and company came rolling into town and took up the challenge of rebuilding. The family was whisked away for a vacation. The fire damaged structure was razed and in typical Extreme Makeover fashion, a beautiful new structure rose from the ashes as hundreds of volunteers, construction workers and the design team went to work 24/7.

We installed the Freedom Climber, helped with dozens of other tasks, and had a chance to see firsthand the inner working of that incredible process of orchestrating the building a house in one week's time. On the day of the family's return, there was still a flurry of last-minute finishing touches going on inside while a large crowd gathered and waited outside to join that clarion call to "Move that bus!" The bus moved and the family melted in disbelief as they gazed upon their new home. All who gathered shared in the celebration. People love restoration. People love to see renewal. People love re-creation.

As humans, we help where we can, but we have our limitations, finite as we are. We can rebuild houses but we can't guarantee a home. We can clear away the charred remains of a structure but we can't guarantee we can clear away cancer cells. We often show up for a week and offer momentary assistance, but we are soon gone and the tremendous task of single parenting lingers.

When we left Pocatello, a family who had been facing great hardships was now on cloud nine as they explored their beautiful new home and tried to wrap their minds around what had just happened. It dawned on us as we headed home that this is the exception, not the rule. In fact this was more of an anomaly than an exception. Most people facing hardships today will still face hardship next month if not next year and the year after that.

Ours is a fallen world. Many bad voices make for many bad circumstances. Many conflicting voices make for many conflicts. Many self-centered voices make for a marginalizing of many. When I steep myself in the woes of the world, or imagine life in a refugee camp or a sweatshop, I can't help but think this world needs a makeover.

When I put myself in the shoes of those needing medical procedures that take them to the point of death or the ceiling of pain tolerance, when I imagine relationships strained to the point of heartbreak, abuses that leave the spirit cowering, I can't help but think this world needs a makeover.

When I think about hardships that become an unbearable burden, when I consider the wreckage that has resulted from sin's entry into the world and the fears and insecurities that death brings, it is impossible to deny that this world needs a makeover.

Jesus, who came to rescue this world, and to offer hope, offers such hope when he says to his disciples:

"Truly I tell you, at the renewal of all things, when the Son of Man sits on his glorious throne ..."
Matt. 19:28

Jesus spoke these words toward the end of his ministry, when thorns and the cross were more immediate than his glorious throne. Yet it was the thorns and the cross that would make his throne glorious, and that would make renewal possible. Jesus spoke these words when a rich young man was wrestling with the voices in head. It was the voice of insecurity that brought him to Jesus. That voice prompted the question:

"What must I do to get eternal life?"
Matt. 19:16

Jesus said in essence, "Shema" i.e. hear and obey:

"If you want to enter life, obey the commandments."
Matt. 19:17

*"Do not murder, do not commit adultery, do not steal, do not give
false testimony, honor your father and mother, and love your
neighbor as yourself."*
Matt. 18:18

These words spoken by Jesus now came into conflict with
other voices in the rich young man's head. In his mind, he
argued that he had kept these commands since his youth.

"All these I have kept," the young man said. "What do I still lack?"
Matt. 19:20

Jesus did not challenge what the rich young man said. Jesus
simply said in essence, "Prove it. Prove that you love your
neighbor as yourself."

*"Go and sell your possessions and give to the poor (according to
Jesus, those in need are our neighbor) . . .
then come and follow me."*
Matt. 19:21

The rich young man left sad because he had great wealth,
and had placed himself first among others. Interestingly, he
came to Jesus wrestling with voices in his head, and now
left with more voices banging around in his head.

Jesus explained to his disciples:

"I tell you the truth, it is hard for a rich man to enter the kingdom of heaven. Again I tell you, it is easier for a camel to go through the eye of a needle than for a rich man to enter the kingdom of God."
Matt. 19:24

(By the way, a camel can go through the eye of a needle. It just needs a little help. You simply break it down into thread size pieces and pass them through. Maybe that is the point. A rich man needs to be broken down. A rich man needs to be reduced.)

The disciples, standing there and watching and hearing this conversation between the rich young man and Jesus concluded:

"Who then can be saved?"
Matt. 19:25

Jesus replied:

"With man this is impossible, but with God all things are possible."
Matt. 19:26

My sense is that the conflicting voices in the world complicate salvation to the extent that we are forced to ask, like the disciples, "Who then can be saved?" Salvation seems impossible. Salvation, even in the most impossible of situations, has always been a possibility with God. The prophet Jonah found that to be true. Jonah had conflicting voices in his head. God had said, "Go to Nineveh." The voices in Jonah's head said, "Take a cruise." The cruise ship ran into bad weather and you know the story: Jonah gets thrown overboard. From the belly of the great fish, in the midst of that darkness, in the midst of that judgment, Jonah cried out:

> *"Salvation comes from the Lord."*
> *Jonah 2:9*

Peter asked one final question as the rich young man disappeared from view:

> *"We have left everything to follow you! What then*
> *will there be for us?"*
> *Matt. 19:27*

Jesus said:

> *"I tell you the truth, at the renewal of all things, when the Son of*
> *Man sits on his glorious throne, you who have followed me will also*
> *sit on twelve thrones. ..."*
> *Matt. 19:28*

Peter, in the midst of "with man this is impossible," sought a glimmer of hope. Jesus offered more than a glimmer by speaking of a time coming when all things would be renewed. The question that arises is this: what is the scope of that renewal? Are we at liberty to believe there is a future renewal that truly touches all things?

The rich young man's priorities needed a makeover.

The Pharisees' and Sadducees' theology needed a makeover.

Sinners and tax collectors needed a makeover.

The lame and the blind, the deaf and the diseased, the possessed and the powerful needed a makeover.

The common people with their conflicting voices needed a makeover.

Those Jesus came to seek and to save, the lost of humanity, they needed a makeover.

A renewal of all things—does this speak of an Extreme Makeover: Humanity Edition?

Dare we imagine the false voices gone?

Dare we imagine conflicting voices gone?

Dare we imagine the voices that call for revenge gone?

Dare we imagine the voices that call for putting oneself first gone?

Dare we imagine the voices that pull us continually away from God gone?

Dare we imagine a true voice now ringing solo in our ears? Dare we imagine peace and the joy that accompanies? Dare we imagine a state of selflessness that bears fruit unimagined? Dare we imagine walking with God?

When Jesus speaks of renewal it is in the context of his enthronement. Yet even at the outset of his ministry, there were signs that things were going to be restored. Take his very first recorded miracle. Jesus and his buddies were at a wedding. It was undoubtedly a wedding with an atmosphere similar to the weddings we attend. Hearts were light. Cares had been checked with the topcoats. Smiles were worn by everyone. The groom indicated his intention to take his bride as his partner and they became one. The ceremony gave way to reception and the merriment began.

At some point as the forks were dinging on the wine glass, Mary, Jesus' mother, noticed the pitch was too high. Were those glasses empty? She investigated and sure enough the wine had run out, one of those logistical glitches. The men were ready to go down to the local distributor and get some cases of beer, but Mary thought it best to keep things elegant. She shared the dilemma with Jesus who, behind the scenes, caused the merriment to flow again by converting water into wine. This was the first miracle Jesus performed, a fitting first miracle.

This miracle made clear what Jesus was all about. Jesus is about conversion, and about restoration. At the outset it was clear that even the elements were subject to this one sent from Heaven. From the outset all in attendance were shown to benefit from his coming amongst us.

Just as Jesus converted the water into wine, so he came to convert a rebellious people into a reconciled people. Think of it in this light: he was communicating at the outset of his ministry the very nature of his ministry. His work was and is to change things. And there will be a culmination of his work at the renewal of all things.

Inasmuch as the scriptures are God-breathed, they have a life quality to them. They are living. That is why when we go to the Gospels we find ourselves in the stories. Jesus prepares mud and puts it on our eyes and we see things more clearly. He commands, "Take up your mat and walk," and we feel empowered to move forward with new energies.

We reach out weary of our weakness and touch his garment, and we immediately feel strengthened. We lie motionless as in a grave, and Jesus calls out, "Lazarus, come forth!" and we hear our name. I hear "Terry!"

His is a work of renewal. He makes things over. He came to restore things. His work is extreme.

Conversion was bound up in every encounter he had. The original intent was that man walk with God in spirit and in truth. Jesus came to restore things to that state. Man had lost his way, the Way was now clear. Man was sinking and in need of a savior, the Savior was now near.

Jesus had not spoken ambiguously about his mission. He had come to seek and to save the lost. He had come to destroy the work of the devil. He had come to draw all men unto himself. He had come as Savior of the world. Jesus had come to take away the sin of the world. This was the work the Father gave him to do, this is what he would do. His is a good work. At the end of the day I anticipate a good ending, simply because that is who he is.

We all recognize good. Place a wrecked car next to a new car and ask a three-year-old which is better and she will point to the new car. I would rather have my eyes examined than my teeth. I am eager for dentistry to take things to the next level, where they do their thing without scraping and picking and prodding and wanting to chat while they ask me to imitate a snake readying itself to swallow an egg.

I prefer the eye examiner's chair. No bright interrogation lights in your face. They ask simple question that require one syllable replies, usually A or B. I especially like it when the instrument in front of my face is toggled between two settings, with the chart on the distant wall being either blurry or crystal clear, and I am asked which is better, A or B? I always get those answers right. I have always loved answering questions correctly. Yet as we get to the fine tuning part of the exam, sometimes it is hard to tell the difference. The options are so close that I feel conflicted. But eventually the correct prescription is determined, and I leave with a clearer view of the world because I was able to determine which view was better.

If I were given the following scenarios and asked to identify which would be the better, I would not be conflicted.

- (A) A train crashes. All are injured severely. Triage is set up. 10% survive, 90% perish.
- (B) A train crashes. All are injured severely. Triage is set up. All recover from their injuries.

B is better.

- (A) Meningitis spreads through a middle school, affecting all 483 students. 10% recover, 90% perish.
- (B) Meningitis spreads through a middle school, affecting all 483 students. All recover.

B is better.

- (A) Sin enters the world through one man and spreads to all. 10% are helped and recover, 90% perish.
- (B) Sin enters the world through one man and spreads to all. All are helped and recover.

B is better.

(A) The year is ES 2011 (that is 2,011 years into the Eternal State). One-tenth of all humanity, roughly 10 billion souls, is blissfully enjoying the New Jerusalem that came down from Heaven 2,011 years earlier. Not a tear can be found, joy abounds and this happy company move about freely in the light of God's presence. Elsewhere, in another domain, nine-tenths of all humanity, roughly 90 billion souls, are tormented by conditions that pain the body, soul and mind. They are bound to this darkness and alienation.

(B) The year is ES 2011 and all of humanity is blissfully enjoying the New Jerusalem that came down from Heaven. Not a tear can be found, joy abounds and this happy company move about freely in the light of God's presence.

B is better.

This is the good ending I anticipate resulting from Jesus' good work. I have been around long enough to anticipate the response that is formulating in the minds of many readers. "This writer is a universalist." I am familiar with universalism, and I am not a universalist. I am a Christian who believes Jesus is the Savior of the world. My emphasis is on the means to the end, not the end. I see regeneration as the work Christ came to do. I believe in the renewal of all things because the Bible speaks of such an end. I would call myself a "thorough renewalist." I see the heart of God as being such that He so loved the world that he gave his one and only Son. I see God's will as being that none should perish, but all come to a knowledge of the truth. I see the work of Jesus, his death on the cross, as satisfying the just demands of God and providing atonement for sin. And I see God as sovereign and able to accomplish his will.

Jesus willed that the water bend and become wine and the water bent and became wine. Jesus willed that I follow and I follow. If God wills that all his works shall give him thanks, then we are safe in looking toward the heavens and declaring:

> *"All your works shall give thanks to you, O Lord."*
> *Ps. 145:10,16,21*

If God wills that all the ends of the earth shall remember and turn to the Lord, and all the families of the nations worship before him, then we are safe in looking toward the heavens and declaring:

> *"All the ends of the earth shall remember and turn to the Lord; and all the families of the nations shall worship before him."*
> *Ps. 22:27*

And if God wills that from the new moon to the new moon, all flesh shall come to worship before him, then we are safe in looking toward the heavens and declaring:

"From new moon to new moon, all flesh shall come to worship before me, says the Lord."
Isa. 66:23

My Facebook experience was short-lived. It reminded me of my experience with my cousin's pogo stick. Everyone else seemed to catch on and enjoy it while I just couldn't get the hang of it. However, Facebook did give me that brief moment where the entire world, if they wanted to, could learn about my religious convictions. In my section under religious views, I had written:

" I believe something really big is going on here."

I still believe this. And I mean really big—as in "the renewal of all things" big!

5 JESUS, THE OBEDIENT ONE

Sometimes we take the liberty to describe a conversation we imagine occurred between other parties. I imagine a conversation within the Godhead that went something like this:

The Father to Jesus and the Spirit: "The human race has made a mess of things and they need help, big time help, soteriological help."

Jesus and the Spirit to the Father: "We are on it, consider it done."

The most frequent designation that Jesus used for himself was "Son of Man." It really was his answer to the question, "And who do I say that I am?"

"Man" was that ideal the human race was created to actualize, to realize and to manifest. "Man" was created in the image of God. God passed to "Man" some of his very own attributes and aspects of his nature. Man in nature was relational. Man in nature was spiritual. Man had intelligence, volition, and emotion. Man was able to commune with God and others. God communicated and Man understood. God expressed joy and Man was capable of sharing that joy. God gave Man dominion over the physical world and Man had the faculties to create, nurture and render productive that world. God called upon Man to "shema" -- that is, to hear and obey. Man, being volitional, was capable of obedience and of experiencing all the peace and security that comes from centering oneself in the will of God.

Adam was a son of Man. He came from that ideal. But Adam fell short of the ideal. Adam fell short of the glory of God. Adam chose other voices and found himself in an environment where it was hard to form an accurate opinion of God. His movements were hampered by garments of animal skin. Things were blurry, as if seeing poorly in a mirror, an out of focus reflection. Man could not see clearly what man was meant to be. Man now found that God was not so near. Other voices now rang louder. Shema was hard. Disobedience was the rule and not the exception. Man was marred.

Jesus came because humanity needed the ideal. Jesus came because atonement needed the ideal. For millennia, humanity had been aliens, lost in space and time. There were none righteous, not even one. Jesus came and lived that ideal life, that righteous life. Jesus came and was the Son of Man, representing the ideal. God spoke, and Jesus obeyed.

A question arises in Christology, and it goes like this: "Could Jesus have sinned?" You would think there are only two possible answers, but somehow many explanations have been offered up. Whenever you get a lot of answers you have to conclude, "This must be a difficult question." I find difficult questions difficult, so I look for other questions that are easier to answer. With this question I simply change the letter "c" of "could" with a "w" and allow the question to be, "*Would* Jesus have sinned?" I like that question, because I feel confident my answer is right. The answer is "NO." Jesus would not have sinned. He himself stated he had come to do his Father's will. He had come as the Son of Man. He had come to show us what it is to be Man, what it is to be created in the image of God, what it is to heed one voice though other voices ring out.

Jesus came as Logos. He came as Word. He came as a clear true voice, representing God, revealing God and raising the notion of "Man" to its intended state. He not only revealed the Father; Jesus revealed Man.

Yet Jesus' mission was not primarily to set before humanity a manifestation of the ideal man. His mission was sacrificial, vicarious in nature. His mission was redemptive. His mission was to make atonement. He was to intervene and propitiate (satisfy) justice's demand that sin be judged.

I live in the heart of Amish country in southeastern Pennsylvania, in a little town called Strasburg. Amos is my Amish friend who helped me when prototyping my invention. The hissing glow of the gas lantern in his machine shop cast things in a different light. I would come into the shop anxious, eager to get beyond the prototyping stage. I'm not sure Amos knows eager. Amos punches a different time clock than me. Somehow my eagerness to move beyond prototyping and to have my invention out in the marketplace faded as we got lost in the tasks of prototyping and fabricating.

Amos is a great fabricator. Give him a set of rough drawings with accurate measurements, and he will produce parts that work perfectly to bring all the mechanical components into a smooth and efficient relationship. But Amos is also inclined to look for alternative ways of doing things. Perhaps it is part of the Amish way, where life is lived with a different perspective, at a different pace and moved along by different principles. Regardless of why he sees things differently, he more than once looked at my drawings and designs and asked the question, "What if we …?"

Amos usually prompted us toward better ends. I came to love it when Amos would say, "What if …?" Even when the "What if …?" proved that an option under consideration was not as viable as we thought, at least we knew the option had been put to the test.

I admire people who ask "What if …?" I guess it goes without saying that many of the advances we realize in practically every area of life are rooted in someone having asked this question.

There are, however, areas of life where the question, "What if …?" is not so welcome. Traditions are not especially welcoming of that question. You can prove it yourself. Next time Thanksgiving comes around, raise the question, "What if we just order pizza for Thanksgiving this year?" And of course, some traditions are less flexible than others. The traditional views of the church are particularly reluctant to entertain "what if" questions. I am somewhat sympathetic with the church's position. It has the burden of preserving and proclaiming ancient propositional truths to a modern world that moves at the speed of light and the click of a wireless mouse, the burden of standing between God and humanity and pointing toward Heaven while warning of Hell.

And institutions, like the church, out of necessity need to put in place creedal, codified and systematized doctrinal statements about what they believe and why they exist. As a young Christian I found comfort in those creedal, codified, and systematized doctrinal statements, and in fact still do in some measure. But what do you do when your journey and experiences raise questions that the Church doesn't answer satisfactorily?

What if you take the liberty to ask, What if...? Here are some of the "what if...?" questions I ask: What if Jesus came to obediently gather unto himself all of humanity's disobedience, and submit it to God's just demand that the disobedience be judged? What if the disobedience that brought sin and death to all of humanity was countered by the obedience that brought righteousness and life? What if Jesus came to gather up all the damage that resulted from the false voices and show how one solitary true and faithful voice could counter the rebellion and offer hope of renewal?

Jesus died because the wages of sin is death. He who knew no sin became sin and the wage was due. But Jesus came to life again because obedience always yields life, triumphant life. The power of disobedience and the damage of the false voices could not prevail over the power of obedience and the healing of the One True Voice. This was the work the Father gave him to do, and the glory of God is centered in this work. If our opinion of God is shaped by this work of

Christ, so that it is our opinion that Jesus is the Savior of the world, not just potentially but really, there is glory bound up in that opinion. Jesus came to do the Father's will, to seek and to save that which was lost.

For me, it boils down to the efficacy of Christ's work. It boils down to this: did his coming and his dying accomplish the desired effect? As I read the scriptures, I sense God desired that sin be taken away. John the Baptist said this rather plainly as he announced:

> *"Look, the Lamb of God who takes away the sin of the world."*
> *John 1:29*

As I read the Scriptures, I sense it was desired that Jesus save the lost. Jesus said it himself:

> *"For the Son of Man came to seek and to save what was lost."*
> *Luke 19:10*

Jesus' obedience produced an effect, and was set in contrast to Adam's disobedience. Adam's disobedience produced an effect. The Apostle Paul draws up this contrast in Romans.

> *"For just as through the disobedience of the one man (Adam) the many were made sinners, so also through the obedience of the one man (Jesus) the many will be made righteous."*
> *Rom. 5:19*

Various groups have done surveys in which they randomly ask questions that are meant to identify those who see themselves as born again. These groups have concluded that the number of born again believers in the world is roughly 10% of the total population. I have no reason to dispute this number. With a current population at seven billion, that means there are six billion, three hundred million unbelievers. That means, if the traditional church's explanation about the destiny of unbeliever is true, then six billion, three hundred million souls would be gathered under the work of Adam and seven hundred million would gather under the work of Christ.

In this scenario, the efficacy of Christ's work is 10%, while the efficacy of Adam's work is 90%. I have a problem with that. It just makes sense to me that Jesus is greater than Adam, that obedience is greater that disobedience. It just makes sense to me that truth trumps falsehood and life trumps death.

What if that is what Paul meant when he said:

"Consequently, just as one trespass resulted in condemnation for all people, so shall one righteous act result in justification and life for all people."
Rom. 5:18

I know that many will urge me to go back to verse 17 and plug in a very essential part of the equation. There Paul says:

"For if, by the trespass of the one man, death reigned through that one man, how much more will <u>those who receive</u> God's abundant provision of grace and the gift of righteousness reign in life through the one man, Jesus Christ!" Rom. 5:17

I stated early on in this book that I believe we are saved by grace through faith. I believe that only those who receive God's abundant provision of grace and the gift of righteousness will find themselves rightly related to God. But I am one of those who believe that faith is not from yourself—it is a gift from God. And as John noted in his Gospel, we become the children of God … not by a human will, but are born of God.

What if God, as it says in the New Testament,

"…is patient with you, not wanting anyone to perish, but everyone to come to repentance."
2 Pet. 3:9

What if Jesus really meant it when he said:

"And I, when I am lifted up from the earth, will draw all people to myself."
John 12:32

What if he really meant "all people?" Not "all kinds of people," as some have suggested, but "all people," as he stated.

Christianity is about faith. Somehow faith factors into the equation. So where does faith come from?

6 FAITH

When we lived in Kenya we had access to two channels on our TV. They both broadcast from Nairobi, which was an hour away, and if you pointed your antenna in the right direction you could get a rather decent picture. The programming was mostly British. CNN news was the international version. On the evening of September 11, 2001, we were getting ready to have supper with the Tolans. Just as they arrived, someone noticed on the TV a "Breaking News." The story being reported was happening live mid-morning in New York City. Planes were crashing into tall buildings. The story began to expand in scope as other locations became scenes of numbing events.

Recently, after almost a decade, the terrorist behind the attacks was killed in a covert operation undertaken by U.S. Special Forces in Pakistan. Osama bin Laden was probably the most notorious terrorist in the minds of this current generation.

History has a long list of terrorists and bad guys, names we would not want for our grandsons. Names like Attila, Pol, Vlad, Ivan and Adolf. But the worst of the worst is a very common name. I am pretty sure I could name thirty people with the name Paul.

The church has canonized Paul, and so we fondly call him Saint Paul. He saw things otherwise. Paul considered himself the worst of sinners.

> *"Here is a trustworthy saying, that deserves full acceptance: Christ Jesus came into the world to save sinners —*
> *of whom I am the worst."*
> *1 Tim. 1:15*

Since I believe Paul regarding the other things he has said, I believe him in this regard as well.

The fact is that Paul was a terrorist. Paul was terrorizing and attempting to eliminate a people group he was prejudiced against. His goal was not to topple tall buildings but to topple this young structure called the Church. His passion was to eliminate the early community of believers, his attack was on the very foundation of the Church.

The fact is, had Paul been successful in his mission to annihilate those involved in this movement called the "Way," all the lives that have been touch by Christ, all the individuals who have come to know newness of life, all the people who have been changed and who have brought forth good works that glorify God, all of the positive impact that Christianity has had on the world for the last two thousand years—all of this would never have happened.

Perhaps Paul, after his conversion, seeing the impact the Gospel was having on his own life, seeing the impact it was having in the world, realized, "I tried to snuff that out, oh what a wretch am I." Perhaps Paul saw his ambitions to silence the Gospel for what it was, an attempt to quiet this "good voice." Paul saw his actions as meriting the title "worst of the worst," "chief among sinners."

I like Paul's conversion. For me, seeing Paul being saved makes it possible for me to accept the fact that God could save anyone. If God can take the worst of the worst and turn the lights on and bring him to knowledge of the truth, then that grace and encounter is sufficient for one and all.

I think the call of Paul is meant to keep us from neatly explaining how faith occurs. Paul was not seeking God. Paul was not even confronted with the Gospel he would later define. Paul was confronted with himself. What happened was, the worst person on the planet had an encounter with God in which he suddenly found his life set against the bigger picture. Paul was enabled to see his life as seen through the eyes of God; he had a moment where he knew as he was known.

The story unfolded like this: the church had been making steady gains. The Jewish authorities were not sure what to make of it or how best to deal with it. Paul was the zealot amongst them. It was plain to him what needed to be done. In Paul's mind, these followers of the "Way" were deviant Jews who were straying from the traditions handed down from generations past. He was zealous for those traditions. He felt it was his part to preserve these traditions even if it took persecution to bring it about.

Paul had sought and secured letters of authority from the high priest to track down these infidels and take them as prisoners. In his mind they needed to be brought back to Jerusalem where they would meet the same fate that befell the disciple Stephen.

"While they were stoning him, Stephen prayed, "Lord Jesus, receive my spirit" … And Paul was there, giving approval to his death."
Acts 7:59

Paul believed that more of these stonings were needed. Perhaps then this mini-revolution would end, and Israel could go back to being a God-fearing nation.

Paul had received letters from the high priest. He was about to receive light from a higher priest. Paul had received letters to oppress and condemn, not knowing that he himself was about to be sent on a mission to deliver letters that would set at liberty those caught up in a greater rebellion.

As Paul neared Damascus, his destination, Paul the persecutor met Jesus the prosecutor. It was a sudden encounter. In a moment Paul found himself on the stand. No time to be sworn in, just an environment that demanded the truth, the whole truth and nothing but the truth. Paul in the brightness of that moment, gave no thought to justify his behavior but humbly identified his confronter as Lord. The light shown so brightly that it was as if he had been laid bare before Him to whom he had to give an account.

> *"As he neared Damascus on his journey, suddenly a light from heaven flashed around him. He fell to the ground and heard a voice say to him, "Paul, Paul, why do you persecute me?"'*
> *Acts 9:3-4*

Paul's initial belief was simply that this voice was worthy of his subjection.

> *"Who are you, Lord?" Paul asked. "I am Jesus,*
> *whom you are persecuting ..."*
> *Acts 9:5*

Paul opened his eyes but saw nothing. Paul had come under the judgment of God. Paul was told by the Lord that he was to go into the city and await further instruction.

> *"Paul got up from the ground, but when he opened his eyes he could*
> *see nothing. So the men traveling with him led him by the hand*
> *into Damascus. For three days he was blind,*
> *and did not eat or drink anything."*
> *Acts 9:8-9*

Paul was moved to darkness before a greater seeing would result. I think I would like to put an asterisk here. Or maybe put that in bold print. Or maybe repeat it. Or maybe all three :

* Paul had come under the judgment of God and was moved to darkness before a greater seeing could result. And out of that encounter faith was born.

Abraham, too, that father of faith, was not an individual searching for God—at least as far as the text goes. He seemed to be minding his own business in Ur when God interrupted things, calling him to leave the familiar for the unfamiliar. God made a promise, Abraham felt this voice rang true and he responded by packing up the YouHaul and heading west then south to Promise Land. The promise was personal and he held tight and thus became the father of faith.

Faith is hard to explain. Why is faith exercised by some and not by others? Why do I believe, and my cousin does not? What gives me confidence to embrace the promises of God while my neighbor has no such confidence? What inclines me to align myself with the teachings of Jesus while hundreds of millions align themselves with Buddha or Mohammed?

I have concluded that faith is hearing a call. I have concluded that faith is receiving the light. Faith grows out of regeneration, that process where divine energy begins to animate areas of life that have lain dormant. I have concluded that regeneration is a work of the Spirit of God that sets us on a trajectory of becoming like Christ. Faith moves the believer in directions toward what we were originally intended to be—a people in fellowship with God. I am pointed back toward the garden, and am given ears to hear the One True Voice.

God comes to us in any number of ways, and we see more clearly than ever before who he is and who we are. We hear more clearly than ever before his invitation to come into the fold and identify with the way of the fold. And the way of the fold is this: "Enjoy the pasture, heed the shepherd and want not." As lost , we welcome the call.

But if it is as simple as that, why aren't more people followers? Why don't more people own Jesus Christ as Lord and Savior? The only explanation that makes sense to me is the doctrine of predestination.

Did you feel that? Did you feel the hair on the back of your neck begin to rise? Did he say predestination?

I remember asking my students at Rift Valley Academy how many believed in predestination. Most said they did not. I told them they had to if they wanted to pass the class. Not really, but I did tell them they should look into it since the scriptures teach it.

Predestination is a hard teaching. Predestination causes the hair to rise on the back of many necks. But predestination has taken on a life of its own, a life somewhat disconnected from the scriptures. Mention it and immediately people begin to think of a teaching that says certain people will go to heaven and the rest will go to hell. It is all predetermined; happy are the elect and cursed are the non-elect.

Predestination goes counter to our notions of free will; we like to see ourselves as autonomous, and fancy the idea that we can determine our own destiny. That is until we come up short of the destiny for which we were hoping. Personally, I find myself less and less excited about this free will thing. The things I ought to do, that I will to do, I don't do and the things I ought not to, that I will not to do, I do. It seems to me that my will is not so free after all, as if the destinies I fancy are too often fanciful.

But what if we limit our understanding of predestination to what the scriptures say? What if we limit its meaning to that divine, sovereign call to some individuals in this life to conform to the image of Christ?

"For those God foreknew he also predestined to be conformed to the likeness of his Son, that he might be the firstborn among many brothers."
Rom. 8:29

What if predestination is about God always maintaining a witness among humanity?

What if in the midst of this great dis-hearing amongst humanity, amidst this rallying to other voices, this being given to disobedience, what if God would have in the midst of the rebellion a number who are given to hear that True Voice? What if predestination and election are about those who in this life are called to "shema"?

What if predestination is about God extending to some the call to be sons through an adoption? We trace our heritage and bent frames back to Adam. Now there is an offer to come into a more secure and loving filial environment.

What if this elective call is to be "Man," as in "Man" who was created in the image of God?

What if it is a predestining call to be "Man" as in "Son of Man," and to conform to that image and thus conform to the image of original intent? What if it is God's will that this witness, this testimony of an elect people heeding the True Voice, runs parallel with a company given to the false voices? What if those given ears to hear the greater voice run parallel with those subject to the lesser voices?

What if the elective calling, which certainly touches on salvation, does not exclude others from salvation, but rather only excludes them from salvation here?

I have room in my theology for God to work throughout the ages. We will look at "the ages" in the next chapter. I have room in my theology for God's judgments to be unsearchable.

> *"Oh, the depth of the riches of the wisdom and knowledge of God!*
> *How unsearchable his judgments,*
> *and his paths beyond tracing out!"*
> *Rom. 11:33*

I have room in my theology for God to be so sovereign that he has space in his redemptive purposes to give all over to disobedience if that giving over is for his glory.

> *"For God has bound all men over to disobedience so that he may*
> *have mercy on them all."*
> *Rom. 11:32*

In the Old Testament, Israel was commanded to go out into the fields at the beginning of the harvest and bring back a sample of the produce. It was a ceremony where they held the sample high before the community to show everyone what was soon to come. This sample from the fields was called "firstfruits."

James speaks of the elect, the chosen, as firstfruits.

> *"He (God) chose to give us birth through the word of truth, that we*
> *might be a kind of firstfruits of all he created."*
> *James 1:18*

I have room in my theology for God to predestine some to be firstfruit. I have room for the elect to be a sample of a greater harvest to come. I have room in my theology for Christ, in his resurrection, to be a sample of a greater resurrection in the future.

> *But Christ has indeed been raised from the dead, the firstfruits of*
> *those who have fall asleep. Since death came through a man,*
> *the resurrection of the dead comes also through a man.*
> *For as in Adam all die, so in Christ all will be made alive. But each*
> *in his own turn: Christ, the firstfruits,*
> *and when he comes, those who belong to him.*

"The spiritual did not come first, but the natural, and after that the spiritual. The first man was of the dust of the earth, the second man from heaven. As was the earthly man, so are those who are of the earth; and as is the man from heaven, so also are those who are of heaven. And just as we have borne the likeness of the earthly man, so shall we bear the likeness of the man from heaven."
1 Cor. 15:20-23, 46-49

Predestination for me is woven into the past, the present and the future. With respect to the past, it explains the covenant relationship Israel alone had with God. In the present, it explains the covenant relationship the church alone has with God. For the future, it explains the renewal of things, as it will be heard in heaven:

"Now the dwelling of God is with men, and he will live with them. They will be his people, and God himself will be with them and be their God. He will wipe every tear from their eyes. There will be no more death or mourning or crying or pain, for the old order of things has passed away. He who was seated on the throne said, 'I am making everything new!'"
Rev. 21: 3-5

7 MOKUSATSU

At the end of World War II, late in July of 1945, Suzuki, the Premier of Japan, was presented with the ultimatum: "End the fighting or else!" The "or else" was briefly explained in the ultimatum's document called the Potsdam Declaration. It was a document representing the voice of the Allies and their war machine, which was now free from its engagement with the Germans who had surrendered a few months earlier. Those operating this war machine had new resolve. The declaration referenced the German surrender and noted that the surrender only occurred as they, the Allies, had flexed their collective muscles against the resisting Nazis and:

"... necessarily laid waste to the lands, the industry and the method of life of the whole German people."

The Potsdam Declaration warned Japan:

"… the full application of our military power, backed by our resolve, will mean the inevitable and complete destruction of the Japanese armed forces and just as inevitably the utter devastation of the Japanese homeland."

Having heard of the declaration, Suzuki and his cabinet were deliberating what their response should be. At a news conference where he was asked about the ultimatum, Suzuki offered the word "mokusatsu," which can be translated at least two ways. Supposedly, Suzuki meant the word to simply communicate "no comment." Those who had the task of translating the response into English chose the alternative meaning, "not worthy of comment."

Those who had drafted the declaration were weary of the war and the prospects of continued casualties. The Allies were simply looking for "We surrender." Anything that smacked of further resistance would be considered provocation. The United States, in particular, was ready to take things to the next level if necessary. That level was 37,000 feet above Hirsoshima in a plane called the Enola Gay with her 9,000 pound payload.

Some have argued that this mistranslation contributed toward the dropping of the atomic bomb. Suzuki's choice of word and the translator's choice in interpretation did add tension to an already tense situation. Had the world been made aware of a Japanese Premier and his cabinet wrestling with the ultimatum rather than seemingly ignoring it, the world and its leaders may have given a bit more space for a Japanese response. If the decision makers for the Allies had known that Suzuki understood the gravity of the situation, and was compiling an appropriate response, continued diplomatic efforts toward ending the war may have ensued and the Potsdam Declaration would have yielded better fruit.

But the "not worthy of comment" translation went to print on July 28, 1945, and the U.S. military decision makers went ahead with plans that had been in the making for some time. Those plans took wings when Col. Paul Tibbets on August 6 boarded his plane named for his mother, Enola Gay Tibbets. Together with his crew and their payload called "Little Boy," Tibbets set his heading for Japan.

What is probably most unfortunate about this moment in Suzuki's life is the fact that prior to and during the war, he was opposed to it. Yet for the many who were supposedly given a glimpse into his heart and mind via that July news conference, the translation of his word "mokusatsu" suggested a stubborn warmonger who defied peace efforts.

The words that make up any language have the potential, when mistranslated, to produce misunderstanding. We have more than one hundred English translations of the Bible or New Testament. We have a thousand books or articles explaining why each is better than the others. Many of these books and articles argue that mistranslations have occurred, leading to misunderstanding for the reader.

There are two words in the Bible that many believe have been translated in such a way that paints a picture perhaps not representative of the heart and mind of the speaker. The two words are commonly translated "eternal punishment."

Imagine if you read in the Gospels a warning from Jesus that those who neglected the poor and needy were to go off for an age where they would be judged by God so that such inaction and neglect would be forever curtailed. Such an act of judgment, for many of us, would be in keeping with a just God who down through the ages has chastened his children.

What translators have given us is a warning in the Gospels from Jesus where those who neglect the poor and needy go off to eternal punishment. For many of us, that seems at a gut level, to be at odds with the God of the scriptures.

The fact that we have accepted the latter translation is mostly due to the fact that this translation has been set before us for the past several hundred years. It is not necessarily the best translation, just the more common translation. It is like the explanation that ordered our solar system around the earth (geocentric) even though a sun-centered (heliocentric) explanation existed. We become amazingly comfortable with the familiar, and sadly will even reach for stones when the familiar is challenged.

The two warnings above differ radically. The first warning paints a picture of judgment as punitive yet purposeful. The second warning paints a picture of judgment as purely punitive. The warning from Jesus comes from Matthew's Gospel and reads like this:

"They ... will answer, 'Lord, when did we see you hungry or thirsty or a stranger or needing clothes or sick and in prison, and did not help you?' He will reply, 'I tell you the truth, whatever you did not do for one of the least of these, you did not do for me.' Then they will go away to eternal punishment, but the righteous to eternal life."
Matt. 25:41-46

Different translations are possible because different meanings can be given to the Greek words that are here translated "eternal punishment." The Greek word "aionios" is translated "eternal" in the above passage. The Greek word "kolasis" is translated "punishment."

"Aoinois" can righty be translated "eternal," but should be understood as the "age of Ages." "Aoinois" corresponds with "aion" (eon), which is safely translated "age". "Aoinois" seems to communicate that time or age which surpasses all previous times or ages. It is the pre-eminent age. It is a time reference where the eternal is front and center, as opposed to this current time or age where the temporal dominates and shapes our lives. It is a God-centered age. The emphasis is on the quality of the age, and not the duration of the age.

"Kolasis" can rightly be translated "punishment," but it is always helpful to see other words and meanings associated with it. "To prune" and "to curtail" are both possible meanings.

Therefore "aoinois kolasis" can be translated "eternal punishment" or (and this is a bit awkward) "the age of Ages pruning" or, equally awkward, "the pre-eminent age of curtailment." It is easy to see why translators went with "eternal punishment."

The point is that "eternal punishment" should be seen as emphasizing the nature of the punishment rather than the duration of the punishment. Our drift toward seeing eternal punishment as that "never-ending torment" that has been preached about for centuries limits a clearer picture of what the words might communicate.

G. Campbell Morgan, who is known in conservative circles as the "Prince of Expositors," touched on this when he warned:

"Let me say to Bible students that we must be very careful how to use the word 'eternity.' We have fallen into great error in our constant use of that word. There is no word in the whole Book of God corresponding with our 'eternal,' which as commonly used among us, means absolutely without end."

Taking the "absolutely without end" dimension from "eternal" allows the word to pick up that aspect of God's nature that is described as eternal. When God reveals himself as eternal, the emphasis is a contrasting of himself with the temporal. It is contrasting his eternal, enduring nature and ways with the temporal, passing nature of earthly things, and the temporal ways in which we conduct ourselves. With God there is no changing, there are no shifting shadows. With men there is much changing. As humans we vary in our ways, our emotions and our purposes. We vary in our judgments, and we vary in our responses.

Jesus warns of eternal punishment, but this punishment will be rooted in that which is absolute—not absolutely without end, but absolutely just. No appeals will be filed. No riots will erupt in the streets. There will be no second guessing the verdict pronounced. This judgment is "God judgment." It is not a separation from God but a separation to God. And as one preacher once warned:

"It is an awful thing to fall into the hands of an angry God."

We live in the midst of the temporal. The systems around us are ever shaped by the limitations that mark the very nature of things. Judgments are rendered with scant evidence. Juries are withheld crucial evidence. Defense teams are allowed to create suspicions that skew judgment. Juries offer their verdicts based on emotions. Judges pronounce their sentences based on current prejudices. This is not meant to slam our judicial system, but only to contrast the temporal nature of the judgments we know with a judgment of God that is only and always fair and just. Eternal judgment has a focus on the nature of the Judge more than the duration of the judgment.

When we shift from eternal punishment as durational and see eternal punishment as "God judgment," there is room for the purposes of God to play out. We have become so accustomed to thinking of eternal punishment as purely punitive and durational in nature that we never even entertain the notion that God's judgment could be remedial as well. His chastening in the Old Testament was purposeful and corrective. His chastening of his church is purposeful and corrective. God throughout the ages has judged men that men might repent and correct their course.

We are told that judgment follows death:

"... man is destined to die once and after that to face judgment..."
Heb. 9:27

The question is, "What is the purpose of judgment?"

8 WARNING

The roads in Kenya can be very hard on tires. I love new tires–even love the smell of new tires. I think if Goodyear came out with a tire-scented air freshener, I would hang it from my mirror. I had just put new tires on our vehicle in Kenya, and was traveling down a rather abandoned stretch of road at about four o'clock in the morning. I wanted to reach my destination by sunrise.

It was foggy, and through the fog I noticed a little lantern sitting by the roadside. It was attempting to illuminate a sign that said "Police Check Point." Police check points were common in Kenya. They all had familiar features: a couple of policeman with rifles, a fire burning with a pot of chai brewing, and two eight-foot-long metal rails with four-inch spikes protruding every couple inches. The two spike-infested rails were strategically placed so that you had to come to a near stop and weave between them. It was while you were slowed down and weaving through them that the police might opt to stop you. If they did, they would check your papers: car registration, proof of insurance, and sometimes they would even want to see a driver's license. On occasion they would like to see a little "paper"—as in money—come back their way.

On this particular morning, the tire-threatening rails were located ten feet beyond the barely perceivable lantern that was attempting to warn me of an otherwise unnoticeable Police Check Point sign. I no sooner saw the sign than I saw the spiked rails. Perhaps if I had been driving a Mini Cooper, and if I had the reaction time of a mongoose, I could have weaved my way through. But my car was not a Mini Cooper, and my family argues that my reaction times are better measured on a calendar than a stopwatch. I turned a hard right into the oncoming lane, but only spared my right tires. Both left tires ran over the spikes and blew out immediately.

I pulled my car to the side of the road, and I remember being disappointed and saddened. I took a deep breath and got out of my vehicle. I looked at the damage and did the math: two flat tires with one spare tire equals a PROBLEM. One of the policemen wandered over to where I was and said, "Pole sana Mbawna," which in this context meant "Too bad for you, Sir." I said something like "Your signage is ill placed, ill lit and inadequate." I may have said something else, but I just can't remember all of the details. The policeman offered me some chai. I wished he had offered me another warning a quarter of a mile earlier, a warning lit by a lantern the size of an elephant, a warning with a blinking light or two.

There are three letters often spoken in those parts: T.I.A., which stand for, "This Is Africa." It is a friendly reminder to all visitors that they are not in Kansas anymore.

Warnings are meant to keep accidents and damage from occurring. Many are ignored. I ignore some. But when I am traveling, I have learned to watch for and heed the warning signs.

Jesus too put up warning signs. They have been in place a long time, and are not hard to understand if you are looking for them. Jesus placed these signs because he knows the threats and obstacles we face. These are not always warnings to keep us safe from harm, but they are always warnings to keep us from becoming detoured or entrenched in ways that cause us to miss the course set before us. Jesus offers warnings so we don't find ourselves stranded and at the mercy of another. The warnings he offered often came with consequences; certain choices would result in certain judgment.

It is impossible to raise your children without issuing warnings. My grandson Reid is two years old, but isn't tall enough to grab the handrail, so we warn him "Go down the steps on your belly, feet first." Noah, my three-year-old grandson, is tall enough for the warning, "Hold the handrail as you go down the steps." My son Michael and daughter Margaret are 23 and 22 years old and enjoy rock climbing. I always tell them as they loads up the Jeep and head off to some one hundred-foot-tall rock face, "Be safe and take your time going up because it's a quick trip down when things go wrong".

When we live our lives in the wrong way, ignoring the warnings, the direction we find ourselves headed is down. When this earthly life ends, and if our life has not been righted, we find ourselves headed to a downward destination. Life is only righted by faith; faith alone puts us in a right relationship with God. The object of faith is Jesus, whom we follow as we move upward in righteousness. When this earthly life ends, and if our life has been righted we find ourselves headed to an upward destination.

For the Old Testament saint, to be absent from the body was to be in the bosom of Abraham, a lovely picture of being safe and in the presence of God, with whom Abraham camped. For the New Testament saint, to absent from the body is to be present with Christ, also a lovely picture of being safe and in the presence of God.

The Bible has different terms for the destiny of unbelievers, those "un-righted" souls. In the Old Testament, the downward destination was the "grave," or Sheol" or "Geheena." The grave suggested "lifelessness." Sheol suggested "a shadowy afterlife of separation." Geheena suggested a "smoldering afterlife of separation amidst unpleasant conditions." To be absent from the body was to be separated from life, goodness and happiness.

In the New Testament, the unbeliever who is absent from the body is also absent from happiness. Jesus warned that the unrighteous and the unbelieving end up in Hades or Geheena or eternal punishment. Often his warning focused more on the consequence than the location. Jesus would tell a parable and warn of choices made that would destine some to a future judgment where there would be weeping and gnashing of teeth. Jesus warned of some going to where the worm never dies, or to a place of fire.

Jesus warned of punishment and spoke of reward. That humanity goes off to reward or punishment after death is undisputable. That the reward and punishment are rooted in justice is also undisputable. Good theology states that the just demands of God will be satisfied. That grace underlies the reward is undisputable. The possibility that grace may underlie the punishment should at least be considered. All humanity must face judgment; what is disputable is the purpose of judgment.

I remember digging the hole to bury my son. I remember filling the hole back in with dirt. As I added the last shovel full to the little raised mound that would settle in time, I saw only a grave. Some call it closure, but I call it "a chapter in an ongoing story." Death is not termination, but a transfer, and I participated in a transfer. From dust we come and to dust we return, but that is only with respect to the physical body. Beyond the transferring of a physical body to the grave there is a transferring of the soul to either Abraham's bosom or to Hell. We learn this from the scriptures, which paint the fuller picture. Our eyes show us the grave, but the scriptures show us the transfer. The grave offers closure, while the scriptures offer hope. It is obvious that the scriptures give us glimpses of the afterlife, and in some instances more than glimpses. But enough is left unsaid that we take up that common task of filling in the blanks.

Noah, my three-year-old grandson, loves playing with trains. I love playing trains with him. Noah particularly enjoys it when I give him a chance to solve a problem. I hold my hand up to my mouth as if I am holding a two-way radio and I lower my voice: "Captain Noah, I'm down here on the Sodor Line and a tree has fallen across the tracks. I was thinking we should have one of the big trains push it off the track. One of the big trains like ... ." (My eyes are looking upward as if I am really thinking hard.) Noah sees me struggling and shouts out, "Gordon! Gordon can push the tree! Gordon is a very useful engine." No sooner has the solution been declared than three-year-old fingers find Gordon and move him down the track toward the Sodor Line. Help is on the way. Problem solved.

Filling in the blanks is what we do. It is what makes life an adventure. The Christian faith has its share of blanks that need to be filled in. We are told, "Love your neighbor as yourself." Our eyes begin looking upward, as we need help with that one. What is that to look like? How should I love my neighbor?

We are told, "Come! Follow me," or "Offer your bodies as living sacrifices, holy and pleasing to God – this is your spiritual act of worship," or, "Hate what is evil, cling to what is good." Those commands leave blanks to be filled in, blanks that require some creative thinking and some resolve. Those blanks touch on the practical. And we begin filling those blanks from the moment we wake up each morning.

It seems to me that the reason we are eager to fill in the blanks is that we sense there is purpose all about us. There is a purpose we move the fallen tree from the railroad track. There is a reason we love our neighbor. There is a reason we are invited to come and follow Jesus. There is a reason we hate evil and cling to good.

Death signals a transfer, and the transfer is toward reward or judgment. Few people toss and turn at night because they are vexed by the prospects of reward. The vexing comes as we wrestle with judgment. In part, the vexing comes because the blanks about judgment have been filled in and the solutions offered still seem devoid of purpose. Judgment as an end in itself does that. Some might respond that the purpose is justice. The unbeliever is getting what he or she deserves. But God seems passive in that arrangement. Man seems to be the determining factor.

If we are certain that God is purposeful, we see purpose in all God does or will do. God will always be about doing good. His holiness and love will find their way into everything that he purposes. Purpose will wrap itself around everything that unfolds Often as things unfold, we find ourselves straining to see what the end will be. We stand at the edge and behold the fringe.

 Job wrestled with events unfolding before him. His soul was vexed having suffered great loss. Friends offered counsel, and he was trying to make sense of their counsel. Job was on the bitter side of "the Lord gives and the Lord takes away." It was a challenging time for Job, yet he recognized that while he suffered, God was at work behind the scenes. God continued to spread out the skies, to suspend the earth and to churn the seas.

> *"He spreads out the northern sky over empty space; he suspends the earth over nothing ... by his power he churned up the sea."*
> *Job 26:7, 12*

These big events put the events of Job's life in perspective. Yet even these big events were really just sideshows.

> *"And these are but the outer fringe of his works; how faint the whisper we hear of him."*
> *Job 26:14*

Though we look only at the fringes, the fringes reveal a great deal about the weaver. There is beauty and purpose in his work. Whether we look microscopically or astronomically at the works of God's hands, his works declare his glory and shout purpose. It is not hard for me to see purpose in judgment. It is not hard for me to see judgment as a means to an end.

There is a parable that suggests this. Jesus told it while talking about forgiveness. In the parable, Jesus communicates that forgiveness is to be a way of life. Peter asks Jesus how many times he should forgive his brother when he sins against him. Peter wanted to know if forgiving seven times represented a forgiving heart. Jesus said:

"I tell you, not seven times but seventy-seven times." Matt. 18:22

Jesus then moved into the parable, which spoke of a king who demanded payment from a servant who owed him a very large sum of money. The servant begged for some time to pay back the money, and the king had pity on him and cancelled the debt. The forgiven servant went out and found a fellow servant who owed him money and he, though forgiven of his debt with the king, still he demanded payment. When the second servant requested time to repay his debt, the first denied the request and had him thrown in prison. When word reached the king he called the forgiven servant before him and said:

"You wicked servant, I canceled all the debt of yours because you begged me to. Shouldn't you have had mercy on your fellow servant just as I had on you? In anger his master turned him over to the jailer to be tormented until he should pay back all he owed. This is how my heavenly Father will treat each of you unless you forgive your brother from your heart."
Matt. 18:32-35

The wicked servant was sent off to judgment, to continue until something was accomplished. The torment was enforced until his debt was paid. This judgment was not an end in itself, but rather a means to an end. If we allow this parable to add to our understanding of judgment, there are certain things we can say. Judgment is punitive; this servant was being punished. Judgment is retributive; this servant was responsible for his debt. Judgment is conditional; this servant was imprisoned until the condition of repayment was met. The parable is told in the context of forgiveness, and the parable ends with a warning that our heavenly Father will treat each of us the same unless we forgive others from our heart. In God's economy, judgment and forgiveness go together. That is the message of the cross. In God's economy, judgment has a purpose.

Because God has forgiven us we should forgive others. That theme is frequently developed in the teachings and stories of the Bible. This parable illustrates that forgiveness should exist among the children of God. The parable also warns us that if we fail to forgive others, our heavenly Father will treat us like the wicked servant, sending us off to judgment until we pay what is owed, until we become what we should be. We owe forgiveness because we have been forgiven. We owe love because we have been loved. God has purposed that we love and forgive. God will bring it to pass.

Judgment in scripture is seldom an end in itself. God in scripture is always portrayed as purposeful. That judgment be considered as purposeful is certainly in keeping with a just and gracious heavenly Father who:

> *"Disciplines those he loves, and punishes everyone*
> *he accepts as a son."* Heb. 12:6

9 HELL – OVER QUALIFIED

I imagined Hell applying for a position in a new translation of the Bible. The editor-in-chief greeted him in the waiting room and escorted him back to his office. The HELP WANTED ad had simply stated, "Looking for qualified word to communicate 'the place and punishment for the unbeliever's afterlife.'" Hell felt good about this interview, because Hell had some experience. The Editor said to Hell, "Please, have a seat and tell me about yourself."

Hell began: "Well, I grew up in northern Europe. My earliest memories go back to around AD 700. Those in my community just called me Hel. I was the word they used to describe the afterlife. I was, in their minds, a misty place, a less than desirable place. I did eventually make my way into the English language. As they began to translate those ancient writings called the Christian scriptures into their vernacular, I seemed a good fit. Of course I came into my own as medieval thinking about the afterlife was transferred to me.

"I was especially influenced by an Italian named Dante, who spoke of an inferno, a complex multi-level realm where unbelievers experienced varying degrees of pain and agony as they were separated from loved ones and God after death. The deeper one descended into the inferno, the greater the pain and agony became. A great deal of artwork flowed from Dante's thoughts, artwork that has come to define me. The medieval imagery still shapes the modern world's understanding of who I am. I have evolved, and am more than was I was initially. I am especially proud of having taken on the attributes of eternity. I plan on being around for a very long time. I bring a lot to the table. I have many references if you are interested."

The editor stood, and from behind his desk extended a handshake and thanked Hell for coming in. He explained there were a few other applicants he needed to consider, and he would get back with Hell shortly. As the door closed behind Hell, the editor instinctively reached for his hand sanitizer, and rubbed his hands together as if trying to warm himself. A cold chill had come upon the room. The editor sat down, pulled up Google and typed "Hell" in the search window. He then clicked on the images button and his screen filled with horrific scenes that caused him to back away and send his cursor to the exit button as quickly as possible.

Hell left the interview thinking, "I have so much to offer."

The editor exited out of Google and called the head of Human Resources and said, "I don't think it is in our best interest to have Hell fill the position. He actually brings too much to the table. Is it possible we just leave the original words in place and let the readers seek out their meaning if they are interested?"

The head of Human Resources asked, "Do you think the readers would do that? How about some footnotes?"

The editor-in-chief replied, "Yes, footnotes are good."

Actually, Hell did get the job, and Hell does bring too much to the table. We read our Bibles and run across the word Hell, and horrific images pop into our head. Most agree we should not lessen the warnings in the Bible, but neither should we exaggerate them. Hell is an exaggeration. The grave is a sober scene regardless of your religious convictions. Shoel speaks of conscious shadowy separation from all peace and safety. Geheena speaks of suffering, weeping, teeth gnashing, fire and soul vexing where the worm does not die. The biblical picture communicates quite adequately that being absent from the body and also being absent from the loving embrace of God is a bad place to be.

For the English speaking world, Hell is part of the language of the Christian faith. We don't need to abandon Hell, we just need to allow the scriptures to define Hell.

When Hell is purely punitive in nature, it becomes a convenient place to project our own despising. We despise the vile and evil and those we deem worthy of severe punishment. Hell is where we wish them. Hell is the place where we can demand two eyes for an eye and two teeth for a tooth. Hell gives us license to hate our enemies.

"Hell," who at the beginning of this chapter was looking for work, will stay plenty busy with the horror movies of today. I think even Dante might be uncomfortable with what Hell brings to the table today. Hell really does need to be revised, and could use some down-sizing. If Hell's job description is to "communicate the place and punishment for the unbeliever's afterlife," Hell should never say more than the scriptures say.

Hell does not have the right to take on a life of its own. We should always remember who holds Hell's keys. Too often we associate Satan with the afterlife realm of judgment. It is essential to remember what Jesus said in the first chapter of the book of Revelation:

> *"And I hold the keys of death and Hades."*
> *Rev. 1:18*

10 EVEN IN HELL WE HEAR VOICES

Water is essential for life. Having lived in Africa seven years, I know how valuable water is. I grew up taking water for granted, assuming it was always readily available. The water of my youth was always clean, just a few steps away. In Africa I saw people walk great distances for water. The water they collected was seldom the clean water I was used to seeing. People involved in water conservation have determined that when the amount of available fresh water drops below 1,700 cubic meters per person per year, the result is water shortage. When this figure drops below 1,000 cubic meters, we speak of water scarcity.

His friends called him Rich because he was rich. People envied him because he was rich. Rich lived a comfortable life, and wanted for nothing. But Rich was not rich in God's eyes. Rich died rich but had to leave his riches behind. He died and went to Hell, and he had no resources in Hell. Hell is not a place of entrepreneurial opportunity, and Rich was now poor and needy. Rich could not change his new status nor could Rich change his environment. Rich was in torment.

Rich would have loved a state of water scarcity. Rich was in an environment of water depravity.

In the Gospel of Luke, Jesus tells a parable. The parable is about Rich, and goes like this:

"Now there was a rich man, and he habitually dressed in purple and fine linen, joyously living in splendor every day. And a poor man named Lazarus was laid at his gate, covered with sores, and longing to be fed with the crumbs which were falling from the rich man's table; besides, even the dogs were coming and licking his sores. Now the poor man died and was carried away by the angels to Abraham's bosom; and the rich man also died and was buried. In Hades he lifted up his eyes, being in torment, and saw Abraham far away and Lazarus in his bosom. And he cried out and said, 'Father Abraham, have mercy on me, and send Lazarus so that he may dip the tip of his finger in water and cool off my tongue, for I am in

agony in this flame.' But Abraham said, 'Child, remember that
during your life you received your good things, and likewise
Lazarus bad things; but now he is being comforted here, and you
are in agony. And besides all this, between us and you there is a
great chasm fixed, so that those who wish to come over from here to
you will not be able, and that none may cross over from there to
us.' And he said, 'Then I beg you, father, that you send him to my
father's house—for I have five brothers—in order that he may
warn them, so that they will not also come to this place of
torment.' But Abraham said, 'They have Moses and the Prophets;
let them hear them.' But he said, 'No, father Abraham, but if
someone goes to them from the dead, they will repent!' But he said
to him, 'If they do not listen to Moses and the Prophets, they will
not be persuaded even if someone rises from the dead.'"

Luke 16: 19-31

Dehydration alone causes many physiological problems.
Lose 15% of your body's fluids and you begin a quick
descent toward death. Rich was thirsty and dehydrated. But
Rich wasn't on the verge of death; he was already dead.
This was afterlife. This was separation from the good life,
from comfort, from security, and from family and
community. Rich's lack of water put him in agony. Water
represents life. Rich was separated from life, at least the life
he was originally intended to live. Rich was a son of Israel,
who owned Abraham as father. And Abraham owned him as

son. God had expectations for Rich; he had communicated through Moses and the prophets how his people were to conduct themselves. God had communicated what life was to look like. Every son of Abraham was expected to live their lives in keeping with God's design. Care and concern for the needy was not just a New Testament expectation:

> *"Share your food with the hungry and provide the poor wanderer with shelter, when you see the naked, clothe him, and do not turn away from your own flesh and blood."*
> *Isa. 58:7*

The Old Testament also taught that:

> *"He who refreshes others will himself be refreshed."*
> *Prov. 11:25*

Rich was far from water. Rich was far from refreshment. Rich was far from life.

During his life, Rich turned away from Lazarus while the dogs turned to Lazarus. Rich lay in comfortable bedding, dressed in comfortable pajamas made of the finest threads while Lazarus laid on the ground at Rich's gate, no doubt in beggars' threads. Rich could only hear the rain falling as it pounded upon his roof, being sheltered from the storms of life. Lazarus felt the rain pound upon his exposed body, being homeless and subject to the storms of life. Rich knew a happy life. Lazarus knew a sad life. Both men came to know death, and death dutifully made its deliveries; Lazarus was carried by angels to the bosom of Abraham, while Rich was routed through the grave to Hell.

Jesus' parables give insight into the issues of life and death. This parable also gives insight into Hell. Some argue we should not make too much of the parables. To me, that is like traveling across the United States, getting to Colorado and reading a sign, "Don't make too much of Colorado." I have never read a parable in which the elements were inconsistent with the world as we know it. When Jesus takes us to an unfamiliar territory like Hell, I expect the elements to be consistent with that world.

Based on this parable, the following can said about Hell:

Hell separates us from the good.

Hell is a place of torment.

Hell has heaven in view, though from far away.

Hell hears faith's voice, though faith is not and cannot be embraced.

Hell is a place for remembering.

Hell is humbling.

Hell provides no opportunity for receiving help from the outside.

Hell provides no opportunity for sending help to the outside.

Hell is where you go when you ignore Moses and the prophets.

Hell is where you go when you neglect the needy.

Hell is judgment and judgment has a purpose. One purpose of Hell is for punitive justice to be handed out. The punitive nature of Hell is described as torment or torture. We are products of our age. Go to the movies and at least one of the sixteen movies being shown will have a horror or torturous theme to it. I have never seen the movie SAW, but I have a good idea what it portrays. We read the words "torment" or "torture" in the Bible, and scenes from SAW or the inferno from the medieval era pop into our heads.

The early church had a different image. It's not that cruelty couldn't be found; crucifixion proved that cruelty was alive and well. Yet the Greek word used in the parable of the rich man and Lazarus portrayed something else. The word is "basano," which meant "touchstone." The word denoted the black silicon-based stone used for testing precious metals by rubbing the metal against it. Metal such as gold left a peculiar mark. Individuals who came under judgmental examination were, in essence, rubbed against the evidence and the facts and that rubbing had a grating effect. That rubbing was tormenting and even torturous. I could see God exposing an individual to a touchstone; I could not see God exposing an individual to the inferno of the medieval age.

Rich died and experienced eternal punishment. The eternal makes a good touchstone. Rub your temporal life against that which is eternal, and there is often a groaning. Rub your fleshly life against that which is spiritual and teeth clinch, sometimes gnash. Rich's life was way too temporal. We all live in time and space, and there will be a temporal dimension to our existence. But we are also children of God, children of the eternal, and that eternal must have its space too. Even here it is good for us to set our lives against the eternal. The contrast helps us to see what our lives have the potential to be and what our lives must be. That is why we are encouraged:

> *If we judged ourselves, we would not come under judgment.*
> *1 Cor. 11:31*

We were created in the image of the eternal. We were to bear that image before the world. Jesus was once asked about paying taxes. He took a coin and asked whose image was on the coin. Those present replied, "Caesar's." Jesus then said, "Render to Caesar what is Caesar's and to God what is God's." The dots that needed to be connected were these: man has God's image stamped upon him, and therefore he belongs to God. And that which is God's is to be rendered to God. As the redeemed we are to set the eternal before humanity. Rich had God's image stamped upon him, yet he hid the eternal by focusing on the temporary. Rich was temporarily rich. Rich stored up no riches in heaven.

Rich died, went to Hell, and came into a touchstone experience that left him tormented.

Rich, in his torment, looked up and saw Abraham far away with Lazarus by Abraham's side. Abraham has always represented faith in the Bible, as he certainly does in this scene. He also represents hope. Nothing suggests Rich was becoming hopeful. Rich was under judgment and was being tormented. Rich's soul felt empty. Rich thirsted. Rich sought pity. Rich felt constrained, but sensed Lazarus had no such constraints. Rich sought pity but pity could not be extended for the Grand Canyon had been placed between Rich and Abraham. An impassable gulf had been fixed between Heaven and Hell. Rich was far from Abraham yet spoke with Abraham and Abraham spoke with Rich. Abraham offered no hope but hope was present.

This parable begs the question, "Shouldn't that be Moses instead of Abraham?" If judgment and Hell are about justice administered to law breakers, shouldn't Moses be speaking to Rich? Yet here we find Abraham.

I believe this parable indicates that in Hell faith speaks, although faith cannot be embraced. Faith too is a touchstone that can cause torment. Rub an unfaithful life against faithful expectations, and guilt and shame naturally surface.

Rich would have loved to lay hold of Abraham even as Jacob laid hold of his night-time visitor at the Jabbok (Gen. 32:24), not letting go until a blessing was given. Rich would have loved to join Lazarus at Abraham's side. Rich felt Hell's constraints, and the most he could hope for was a little relief from Lazarus' fingertip dipped in water. It was a simple request but no such relief was possible, an indication of Rich's humiliation.

I don't like fingers finding their way into my drinking water. I have moved about in some of the worst slums on the planet. Haiti knows poverty and I spent months in Haiti. The Kibera slums of Nairobi break your heart. It is impossible to pass through Kibera without encountering a beggar. Their fingers are not dirty by choice. Yet it would not be my choice to have those fingers deliver thirst-quenching water to me. Rich found himself in such a humbling state that his scruples made room for the finger of beggar Lazarus to deliver water to his tongue. Hell evidently does that to you. Hell evidently humbles you. That might be another purpose of Hell.

Hope for a droplet of water was not realized, yet hope was present. Faith could not be embraced yet faith was present.

While living their lives Rich had much, Lazarus had little. Rich did little with what he had. Lazarus could not do much because Rich never added to his little. Rich was hoping to make a difference now—to have Lazarus go to his brothers and warn them to repent least they join him in his torment. Misery evidently does not love company, at least not true misery.

We aren't told much about Rich. It seems that he saw himself as the center of his own universe. It also seems Rich had little confidence in Moses and the prophets. Abraham told Rich there was no need to send Lazarus to his brothers because Rich's brothers had Moses and the prophets to call them to repentance. Rich evidently sensed that the prophetic voice would ring hollow in their ears, perhaps because that was what Moses and the Prophet meant to him. Perhaps that's the weight Rich gave God's word when he was preoccupied with life. Rich argued that if someone from the dead went to his brothers then they would repent, that witness would be different. Abraham disagreed. Faith knew better.

107

Rich wanted to make a difference now. That hope was not to be realized. Yet hope was present.

Rich had died and gone to Hell. Rich had boarded a ship, ship with a delivery to make. It was a slow sailing ship, and the waters were turbulent. The voyage was nauseating. Rich's quarters were dark and dank. The tiny portal revealed Abraham, but oh so very far away.

11 THE HMS HADES

When Hell's eternal sail is lowered and a purposeful sail is hoist, we find a ship that no longer sails on an endless sea. Instead we find a ship that must make landfall. Hell has a delivery to make. Hell has numbered days.

"Then I saw a great white throne and him who was seated on it.
Earth and sky fled from his presence,
and there was no place for them...
The sea gave up the dead that were in it, and death and Hades
gave up the dead that were in them, and each person was judged
according to what he had done. Then death and Hades were
thrown into the lake of fire.
The lake of fire is the second death."
Rev. 20:11, 13, 14

Put Hell in the service of His Majesty (God), and Hell becomes just another created thing. Created things all have one thing in common; they were created by Christ and for Christ.

"He (Christ) is the image of the invisible God, the firstborn over all
creation. For by him all things were created: things in heaven and
on earth, visible and invisible, whether thrones or powers or rulers
or authorities; all things were created by him and for him."
Col. 1:15, 16

My sense is that most people do not like solitude, at least not prolonged solitude. Many do not even like momentary solitude. The radio is always on in their car. Headphones are always in their ears. The TV is turned on as they move from one room to the next. Text messages keep them connected to others. All of this smothers us with the presence of others, and in others' voices.

I think it is good to be other-oriented. Yet it is also good to value solitude. Jesus valued solitude. Rich now had no choice about solitude.

I have a simple definition for Hell: "Hell is where we are introduced to ourselves." The recorded conversation between Rich and Abraham was short. Abraham offered Rich some explanations and one instruction, which was "remember."

> *"Son, remember that in your lifetime you received*
> *your good things."*
> *Luke 16:25*

If I were in the quarters next to Rich on the HMS Hades, and he slipped a piece of paper through a crack in the boards with the question: "Is this my end?" I would be inclined to write back: "Man's chief end is to glorify God and enjoy him forever."

When our conviction is that this is the chief end of man, that this is what God has purposed, and when our conviction is that man cannot thwart the purposes of God;

then, like the sun and gravity and everything else that makes up the created order, Hell too has a task to perform.

Rich had been created to be loved and to love. If he was like most infants, out of the womb he was received into loving hands. If he was like most children, his parents provided him with security and nurture. That is by design, and we expect it of one another. If there is failure, the larger community will take the child and provide what they need—to love and be loved.

Love is at the root of God's purposes because God is love. Even divine justice is born of love and even limited by love. Love has always been expected, and has never been an option. Divine justice requires that we love God with all our soul and our neighbor as our self. This is the debt we owe.

> *"Let no debt remain outstanding, except the continuing debt to love one another."*
> Rom. 13:8

A conviction that Divine justice will administer whatever discipline is necessary for whatever time is required until love is realized, is simply a conviction that God is purposeful. Like the servant who was forgiven his debt but failed in love to forgive his fellow debtor, all those who fail to love will go off to the touchstone, to the tormentor, until their debt is paid in full. Love is the key. If I were to restate the answer to the question, "What is the chief end of man?" I would simply say, "Man's chief end is to love and be loved."

Love is a major theme in the Bible. For many of us, one of the first passages we memorized from scripture speaks of the love of God:

"For God so loved the world that he gave his one and only Son, that whoever believes in him shall not perish but have eternal life. For God did not send his Son into the world to condemn the world, but to save the world through him."
John 3:16, 17

Love was also a major theme in Paul's writings, which is interesting coming from a man who once breathed out hatred. The change for Paul came when he came under judgment, when he was introduced to himself. It was noted earlier that Paul was, by his own accounting, the worst of sinners. His conversion, from being a man with little pity and less compassion to becoming a man who endured great hardship out of love for others, seemingly required little arm twisting from God. God confronted. Paul changed.

Paul became a man of love as self-interest gave way to self-denial. Paul told the Corinthians:

> *"For I am not seeking my own good but the good of many,*
> *so that they may be saved."*
> *1 Cor. 10:33*

Lazarus could have used a converted Paul in his life. Rich should have been to Lazarus what Paul became to others. Paul was confident this was the way of God and so he encouraged others:

> *"Follow my example, as I follow the example of Christ."*
> *1 Cor. 11:1*

Paul became an expert at love. He came to describe love in such a way that his description is probably quoted more often than any other as people seek to understand true love:

> *"Love is patient, love is kind. It does not envy, it does not boast, it is not proud. It does not dishonor others, it is not self-seeking, it is not easily angered, it keeps no record of wrongs. Love does not delight in evil but rejoices with the truth. It always protects, always trusts, always hopes, always perseveres.*
>
> *" Love never fails. But where there are prophecies, they will cease; where there are tongues, they will be stilled; where there is*

knowledge, it will pass away. For we know in part and we prophesy in part, but when completeness comes, what is in part disappears. When I was a child, I talked like a child, I thought like a child, I reasoned like a child. When I became a man, I put the ways of childhood behind me. For now we see only a reflection as in a mirror; then we shall see face to face. Now I know in part; then I shall know fully, even as I am fully known."

"And now these three remain: faith, hope and love. But the greatest of these is love."
1 Cor. 13:4-13

Paul's words about love came as he wrote to a congregation struggling to implement love in their community. They faced division, behavioral issues and a host of problems that existed because love was lacking. Even the spiritual gifts given by the Spirit for the enrichment of the community were being misused because this community, though rich in their gifts, was not rich in love.

Paul argued that love was the most excellent way. A great deal of what makes up the human experience will pass away, yet love will endure. Much that we focus on, as with the Corinthians, is temporal in nature. Love is eternal. Love is the most excellent way. Man was created to be loved and to love.

Paul also argued that much of the failure we see around us is due to the fact that we know in part, and our ability to speak the truth is partial. We live amidst imperfection. But when perfection comes, the imperfect disappears. Perfection occurs when we see face to face, and we see things clearly. Now we see but a poor reflection as in a mirror, but then we shall see face to face. Now I know in part; then I shall know fully, even as I am fully known.

When I see Paul being confronted by God, I see him being confronted with himself. Paul saw himself as the defender of traditional Judaism, a zealot whose reputation preceded him, who proudly would put an end to apostasy and restore the faith of the fathers. Jesus, however, saw Paul ignoring the ax that had already been put to the root of the tree of traditions. The traditions of Israel represented the old wine. New wine was now here, and new wineskins were needed. The old traditions had served their purpose, and new traditions were being put in place.

Paul had heard it said, "Do not murder, and anyone who murders will be subject to judgment." The new tradition was, "Anyone who is angry with his brother will be subject to judgment." Paul had heard it said, "Eye for eye, tooth for tooth" and "Love your neighbors and hate your enemies." The new tradition called for turning the other cheek and a loving one's enemies. Jesus saw Paul and his traditions as the true apostasy. Plain and simple, in the eyes of Jesus, Paul was an antichrist.

Paul's encounter with Jesus on the Damascus road marked the beginning of his journey toward knowing himself as Jesus knew him. The mirror's dim reflection began to reveal the truer Paul. The face that was clearing up before him was his own face. Not the Paul that Paul knew but the Paul that Jesus knew.

For any one of us, such an encounter has the potential to prime us for greater revelations and greater understanding. To know as we are known is painful. To see ourselves through others' eyes can cause teeth to gnash. To somehow feel the pain we have caused others to feel would surely produce weeping. But it also begins to move us toward love. For where there is humility and a contrite heart, love is not far away. Where there is a sense that the offender has identified with the pain he or she has caused, forgiveness is not far away. Where there is movement toward repentance, reconciliation is possible.

The 1970s British band 10cc opened one of their songs with these words: "Everything you do it comes back to you."

This is certainly a sentiment that is universally acknowledged by humanity. Eastern religions tell their adherents to mind their dharma so as to create good karma. We in the West are told to mind what we sow for that we shall reap. Paul says in Romans that the requirement of the law has been written on every heart.

So what if God ultimately wants me to love? What if God could change my constitution so that it was as natural for me to expend love as it is for me to expend breath? What if the purpose of judgment was corrective? What if the "afterlife" is not an endless extension into eternity, but rather another age just like the ages before, in which God continues to work out his purposes of redemption?

What if, as with the wicked servant who failed to forgive his debtor, judgment is that place where we pay the debt we are responsible for?

We can never satisfy the just demands of God when it comes to the sins we have committed; Jesus alone satisfies that demand. But we are responsible for forgiveness.

Rich sank to the floor of his quarters. It was a place of emptiness. He leaned his back against the wall, finding it hard to get comfortable. On the other side he heard the sound of grinding teeth. He asked, "Is someone there?" A parched reply came back, "My name is Adolf, and my soul is weary. I too have a portal. It is an ever-changing scene. So very many who lie at Abraham's side, whose eyes I must look through. So many whose pain I must feel. So many who ask, 'Adolf, Adolf, why did you persecute me?' So very many who are required to bring me to know as I am known. My teeth are like Israel's sandals that could not wear out in their wilderness wandering. My jaw muscles hurt. My throat is dry yet my cheeks are wet.

"Looking through my portal and seeing Roma has been the worst so far. Looking through Roma's eyes and knowing myself as I was known, I beheld a bastard. Looking through Roma's eyes I saw a monster. Roma was just a girl. Roma felt secure in her community. The gypsies were a close knit bunch. I never saw them for who they were. I despised them for their differences. Roma knew love within her community. I brought hatred to her community. Security disappeared when I came on the scene. I turned everything upside down.

"Roma's father was a strong man, and Roma felt safe when her Dad was near. I felt her confidence in her father and the peace she felt with him. But I changed all that. Her strong father was no match for the ruthlessness I set in motion. Roma felt herself being pulled from her father. I felt Roma being pulled from her father. I saw a monster tearing a

119

community to pieces. I saw what no person should ever have to see. Roma witnessed a darkness that I created. There was no pity, though many voices sought pity. Mercy was alien to the hearts I had shaped.

"Roma saw her strong father put to death before her eyes. I saw this strong father die before my eyes. I felt what he felt, helpless to help his daughter, helpless to help himself. I saw this strong man as my father, I saw it through Roma's eyes, I felt my heart sink through the bottoms of my feet. I saw Adolf and Adolf was a monster. Then I saw a cruel hand grab Roma and I felt the separation and fear that floods into the heart and mind of an innocent eight-year-old girl. Many scenes passed before me, scenes I had to see from many angles, scenes I had to feel through sensibility of many. Time is different here. It is not measured by tics. Time is measured by knowing. I have much knowing yet to do; Roma was but one. I am forever looking up and seeing others. This was one of countless scenes through the portal, and as each change Abraham says "remember".

"I am far from finished here. My teeth will gnash on for a long time to come, and rumor has it that I have yet to see things through the eyes of God. It is appointed unto man once to die and after that the judgment. I have felt no injustice in this judgment. I have felt much pain knowing as I am known. I am continually tormented as I come against the touchstone. The evidence is grating. The testimonies tear me apart. Roma is safe now. I hope Roma somehow knows that I was knowing Adolf as she knew Adolf. I wonder if she could ever forgive me. Can such forgiveness be found?"

Rich pulled away from the wall. He had nothing to say in return. Rich thought to himself, "This could be a long voyage." Rich felt his head being turned toward the portal.

It is six miles from my town of Strasburg to a smaller town called Nickel Mines, Pennsylvania. It was the heavy helicopter traffic that signaled something was up. The helicopters were moving low and fast toward Lancaster city. Clearly something was going on. Usually when you hear multiple helicopters in the air, it is the Air National Guard out on a training mission.

Yet these passengers were not guardsmen. These helicopters were not Air National Guard. These were life flight helicopters, and the passengers were young Amish girls. Hours earlier these girls were moving with grace through another school day in quiet southern Lancaster County. Now they lay motionless, some dead, some in dire need of medical attention, and grace seemed absent. The scene at the school house was horrific. Disbelief rocked the community and the world. But grace was not absent. This story must always be about innocent girls who were shot.

Yet grace has a way of graciously complementing the events of our lives. Even in tragedy, grace remains amazing. Even in the midst of the horrific, grace seasons the most bitter of times. Grace found its way into the aftermath of that October day. In gentle gestures of forgiveness the broken community began to find healing. Before many had time to become angry, forgiveness was already binding up the broken and comforting the bereaved.

When I read about Paul's conversion, I concluded that anyone could be converted. When I read about the Amish grandfather, whose granddaughter lay dead in the aftermath of this shooting, reminding others that forgiveness was the right response, I concluded anyone could be forgiven. I concluded that all of us have the capacity to forgive.

Mention Adolf and Hell in the same sentence and nobody notices. Mention Adolf and Heaven in the same sentence and you would swear there were not that many pitch forks and axes in your county. We don't want to find Adolf in Heaven. Adolf Hitler was a murderous man who caused much suffering. We wouldn't be comfortable with the likes of Adolf.

Paul was also a murderous man who caused much suffering, and who was on a mission of genocide. We expect to see Paul in Heaven. Some of us even fancy sitting down and chatting with Paul. Paul ended up in Heaven because he was forgiven. He came under judgment, he experienced darkness, and he then came to a fuller understanding of things. Paul, the worst of sinners, was gathered up in the gracious salvation of God. God sent his Son not to condemn Paul but to save Paul through him.

Hades is not a place of atonement. The cross was the place of atonement. Hades is a place of retribution. We are responsible for what we are capable of doing. Rich, Adolf, Paul and I are not capable of atonement. We are capable of restitution. We owe love, and love must be paid.

12 KALEIDOSCOPE

A picture is worth a thousand words. If you can't read, a stained glass window is worth ten thousand words.

When you are seated in the sanctuary of St. Michael's Episcopal Church in Orlando, Florida, you cannot help but be impressed with its large circular stained glass window. Twenty-five small circles of stained glass fill in the larger circle. Each of the twenty-five has scenes from the Old Testament. There is beautiful symmetry to the whole. Each scene contributes toward turning outside light into a historical overview of Israel's faith journey. Because it is round, you feel as though you are looking into a kaleidoscope. You can imagine setting up a ladder outside, grabbing the window's outer edge and giving it a turn, and then returning inside to see what new scenes appear. Of course it doesn't work that way.

We go to church and whether there are stained glass windows or not, the church faithfully sets beautiful themes and scenes before us – themes that underpin our faith and strengthen us for the journey we are undertaking. The word is preached and light passes through the message, causing stories to stand out and scenes to become rich with meaning for our lives. We go to church, we sing our songs, we offer our prayers, we celebrate communion, we gather around the Word, we give so that the kingdom might expand and we find ourselves spurred on toward good works. We leave as renewed beings, having experienced light passing through our fellowshipping and adding color to our spiritual world.

Within the Christian community we also find our lives enriched as we seek one another's counsel, bear one another's burdens, wrestle with the issues of life and even wrestle with the doctrines and themes that we find challenging and stretching our faith. We take up questions of faith and we offer our perspective while others recommend possibilities according to their way of thinking. We listen to others as they ask, "Could it be that ...?" or "Maybe the point is ...?" or "What if ...?"

When I get to the chapters of the Bible that deal with final judgment, I ask, "What if...?"   I ask this because I find some of the themes taught by the church about final judgment don't square with my understanding of God.

The book of Revelation is fascinating. Its scenes are from another world and the images are alien to our categories. There are multi-headed creatures, and beings with seven horns and seven eyes. There are locusts that look like horses and wear crowns and have teeth like lions. Songs ring out. Woes are heard. Dragons and beasts threaten the human race. Dragons and beast devour some and befriend others.

John of Patmos wrote the book, based on a vision God gave him. It was a vision of churches and of thrones, of judgment and inheritance. And it was a vision of renewal.

Monsters are depicted because we wrestle not against flesh and blood. Thrones are depicted because authorities are working behind the scenes. Agents of judgment move out from both the camp of good and the camp of evil. John shuttles back and forth between Heaven and earth.

On earth, humankind, who have had a propensity for leaning in the direction of other voices, finds the mother-of-all "other voices" to have surfaced and now dominates these last days. The other voices, the false voices, are becoming more demanding. A rebellion of epic proportions is underway.

Judgment is poured out. The campaign lasts but seven years, at which point a white horse breaks through the clouds. The rider is recognized as faithful and true. He comes against the unfaithful and the false and prevails. He defeats his foes and humanity's foes.

The point has often been made that it is easier to imagine something than to describe it. We can imagine a camel perfectly; describing one, however, takes a special skill set. I think the imagination is a great gift God has given us. When my wife and I were feeling called to go to Africa, we imagined what it would be like to sell our home, pull our three children away from the familiar and relocate our lives far away. We imagined the challenges. We imagined the rewards. We painted a partial picture for our mind's eye, a picture that helped us with the decision-making process.

In the book of Revelation, chapter 20, there are a few verses that describe the final judgment when all souls stand before the throne of God and are judged according to what they had done. It is a scene where our minds naturally take over, and we imagine the events being described. I have certain convictions that I have made known in this book. When I bring those convictions to this final judgment scene, my mind takes those events and I imagine what the scene could be in light of my convictions.

The imagination can be like looking through a kaleidoscope. We see things as we are used to seeing them. Then we use our imagination, and it is as if we reached out and turned the outer cylinder just slightly to make the scene change. We see other possibilities. I aimed my imagination toward the final judgment, gave the outer cylinder a slight turn, the elements within tumbled and my view changed.

Rich thought the voyage upon the HMS Hades would never end. His jaw never stopped aching. His teeth never stopped gnashing. His cheeks never dried, and that worm, oh that worm, and that room next door, oh the groans from that room next door. The voyage seemed to go on forever. As the HMS Hades made landfall it was as different type of landfall; the land and sky fell away.

> *"Then I saw a great white throne and him who was seated on it.*
> *Earth and sky fled from his presence,*
> *and there was no place for them."*
> *Rev. 20:11*

Rich moved forward, surrounded by a throng of people that seemed as numerous as the sands of the seashore. They all looked as weary as him. Other large crowds blended into this throng, and they all made their way instinctively toward a great white throne. It was as if this was an appointment hardwired into their motherboard. Rich found the mood to be solemn. There were familiar faces in the crowd. Rich noticed Lazarus. Lazarus recognized Rich and nodded as a son of Abraham would nod to another son of Abraham. Adolf stood next to Roma. Roma nodded as a neighbor nods to a neighbor. It was as if the damage done in the neighborhood had been repaired. It was as if restitution had been made. Restitution can be paid and one still have other charges pending. The mood was solemn. This appointment had to do with judgment. Everyone knew it. No one asked, "Why are we here?" There was no hint of resistance, and there was certainly no hint of rebellion.

Rich felt disoriented. The familiar was gone. Earth and sky had fled. Rich was not rich here. Rich had seen how poor he was. Rich remembered faintly that he used to be able to justify anything he did. He felt unable here to muster such arguments. This scene had judgment and accountability written all over it. There was no Bible on which to lay your hand and swear to tell the truth, the whole truth, and nothing but the truth. The truth was here. Truth permeated this strange environment. The truth would not depend upon the testimony of man. The truth was bound up in books, books that represented things as they were, books that told the truth, the whole truth, and nothing but the truth, all helped by God.

Rich could not get used to the feeling of disequilibrium. He stood there before the throne but his stance felt different. It was a suspended type of standing. He did not feel grounded, but rather as though he were in the hands of another. The only thing familiar was humanity. But even humanity seemed different. There was a quiet and humility to this throng. Though their number was greater than all the armies that ever marched, there was no hint of marching here. Though history's greatest commanders and leaders were present, there was no voice to command.

This sea of humbled humanity stood between polar realities. Before them stood the great white throne. The throne made it clear that the universe is a theocentric universe. Yet this throne also had a transcendence to it that placed it outside of the universe. There was also a permanency to the throne that brought new meaning to eternal. This throne signaled sovereignty. The temporal had no place here and so the earth and sky fled. No words came from the throne but truth emanated. This throne evoked a sense that it was appropriate for him who was seated on it to receive:

"Power and wealth and wisdom and strength and honor and glory and praise…for ever and ever."

Rev. 5:12-13

Behind the sea of humanity stood a lake of fire. It was obvious that whatever ended up in this lake would never be retrieved. If something or someone fell in or was cast in, even the greatest engineers who ever lived and the bravest souls who ever rescued would not retrieve this lake's victims. Already the lake laid claim to some. The beast and the false prophet had been thrown in at the end of the great tribulation:

> *"But the beast was captured, and with him the false prophet who had performed the miraculous sign on his behalf. With these signs he had deluded those who had received the mark of the beast and worshipped his image. The two of them were thrown into the fiery lake of burning sulfur."*
> *Rev. 19:20*

Satan was thrown in after the final rebellion:

> *"And the devil, who deceived them, was thrown into the lake of burning sulfur, where the beast and the prophet had been thrown."*
> *Rev. 20:10*

Death and Hades, after delivering the dead in them to the throne, they too joined the flames:

"Then death and Hades were thrown into the lake of fire.
The lake of fire is the second death."
Rev. 20:14

The Most High God before them, the lake of fire behind them, no earth or sky to give them their bearing; humanity found itself between the Rock and a hot place. There was nothing comfortable about this moment. And looking at the books to be opened, this was going to be more than a moment.

Aboard the HMS Hades, Rich had been given plenty of time to think. He thought about his life, and about life in general. It was clear that he had fallen short of the glory of God. He had lived his life as he chose. It was his voice that charted his course. He gave little room for the voice of God, or for the voices of Moses and the Prophets. The voices he heeded spoke contrary to the better voice that existed in Israel. The Law was present, but it just wasn't minded much. Rich sensed his problem was not unique to him; all of humanity had allowed the other and opposing voices to impact their lives. The problem has always been that the voices we heed shape our lives.

Rich began to take in the features around him. There was the throne, which represented truth. There was the lake of fire, which represented the false. In fact the vary origins of falsehood and disobedience and rebellion had been thrown into the lake. The Beast and the False Prophet and Satan all came under the judgment of God, and were not to be retrieved ever again. Even death and Hades, those consequences of rebellion and disobedience, joined the irretrievables. Rich felt more connected to that which was in the lake than to that which was on the throne.

The books were easily recognized for what they were: history books. These books were accurate, comprehensive, and they answered the unanswered questions. They knew where Jimmy Hoffa was buried. They knew who shot President Kennedy. They knew Rich's secrets and they knew Adolf's crimes. These were books of deeds.

The Book of Life was different. This book focused on the actions of another, and on life. Rich felt more connected to death, which had come to Rich long before he died. Rich had heeded the voices that led him away from God. These voices were now in the lake of fire, and Rich felt an uncomfortable connection to them. The Book of Life suggested life and it too held a record. There was a universal sense that if anyone's name was not written in the Book of Life then the lake of fire was their portion. The books of deeds would open first.

13 BENDING AND LIFTING

As the books began to open, individual stories flowed into one another. Each story was self-contained, yet each was connected to the stories nearby. The story within a clan became a story within a nation. The individual story became a story of the world. The world's story was being told; one story unfolding with one hundred billion stories connected within it. Separate lives under examination yet one life under examination. This was humanity's story, and humanity's judgment.

Rich and the others, all one hundred billion, could not help but notice how this story was timeless. There was no progression of ages. The recent was somehow woven into the past. Everything was present. Scenes randomly unfolded yet there was purpose to this review. Cain's attack of Abel was seen alongside a saint in Calcutta administering love. Paul's murderous threats overlaid his penning of the thirteenth chapter to the Corinthians. Firemen raced up long stairwells while terrorists slowly made their way up the steps to board a plane. Bombs were dropping on birthday parties. Students took lecture notes while ideologies were being born. Vows were made as the divorce papers were signed.

Rich and the others, all one hundred billion, also noticed their sensibilities were different from the past. An element was missing. They never remembered valuing truth as truth was valued here. Sensibilities of the past always had a true – false conflict going on. Something felt good, and yet in truth it was bad. An action that was profitable was falsely considered a waste. Now it was as if the false was gone, as if the false voice had been silenced. It was as if the false was irretrievable. The lake of fire owned the false voices. This put those actions under review, those scenes from the books, in a different light. Anger was seen as murderous. Vengeance was seen as trespassing. Lust was seen as adultery. Even indifference became criminal. As Rich and others viewed their lives, they all saw themselves as poisoned. They felt as though death had always been in their veins, restricting their breathing, cramping their motions, blurring their vision, slurring their speech. As their lives came into focus, little things became big things and big things became little things. Joys became more joyful and sorrows became more sorrowful. The good seemed better and the bad seemed worse.

Rich and the others, all one hundred billion, noticed a strange phenomenon. Every action taken, every word spoken, every thought ever thought seemed to bend in one of two directions: either toward the throne or toward the lake. Yet there was no sense that things were hanging in the balance. There was no hoping that somehow the good would outweigh the bad. Humanity, as the scenes unfolded, was increasingly identified with the lake. Humanity's history was marked mostly by the other, lesser, and deceiving voices toward which they bent. Humanity now felt bent toward the lake. The lake seemed more fitting than the throne as their due. Teresa felt it. Paul felt it. Rich felt it. All felt it. With sensitivities in tune with the divine, an honest appraisal was under way. Holiness had not defined humanity, either in part or the whole. Holiness was a call seldom heeded. Holiness at best was only a pursuit among other pursuits.

The best of the best joined the masses and owned the fact that "We have all sinned and fell short of the glory of God." As the unfolding continued, this new sensitivity gave rise to longing that more scenes would bend toward the throne. The scenes that bent toward the throne evoked human potential; they spoke of what was meant to be. Each action that had its origin in God and was bending toward the throne was recognized as good and just by these being judged. Each kind and edifying word that was spoken signaled truth, and this crowd could only value truth.

Humanity could see how things might have been if deception and falsehood had never been given space. With each scene that bent toward the light, humanity saw the kingdom of God and the righteousness that brings peace and joy. All saw how life should have been, how it was meant to be. But too many scenes were bending toward the lake. The throne signified life while the lake signified death. With so many scenes bending toward the lake humanity was feeling death. It was as if poison was in their system. There was a sense of dying in this gathering.

There is an account in the Old Testament in which a people found poison flowing through their veins and death was in the camp. The story is about Israel in their wilderness wanderings and it goes like this:

137

"They traveled from Mount Hor along the route to the Red Sea, to go around Edom. But the people grew impatient on the way; they spoke against God and against Moses, and said, 'Why have you brought us up out of Egypt to die in the wilderness? There is no bread! There is no water! And we detest this miserable food!

"Then the Lord sent venomous snakes among them; they bit the people and many Israelites died. The people came to Moses and said, 'We sinned when we spoke against the Lord and against you. Pray that the Lord will take the snakes away from us.' So Moses prayed for the people.

"The Lord said to Moses, 'Make a snake and put it up on a pole; anyone who is bitten can look at it and live.' So Moses made a bronze snake and put it up on a pole. Then when anyone was bitten by a snake and looked at the bronze snake, they lived."
Num. 21:4-9

Israel was on their way to the Promised Land. They possessed the law that was to define them as a nation. They had a history of God's faithfulness and his divine intervention on their behalf. Recalling that faithfulness and those intervening events was to influence their decisions and bolster all future progress. God moved with them and provided for them. God's voice was in their midst, speaking through Moses and Aaron. God spoke to them in any number of ways. The true voice was in Israel. But resistance flows through the veins of the sons of men and rebellion is never far away. Other voices called out in Israel's camp, calling the Israelites to move backward. Israel was longing for Egypt, from which they had been delivered. They had forgotten that Egypt represented slavery; they remembered only the fresh leeks and forgot about the forced labor.

Some of God's object lessons can be painful, and Israel was about to find out just how painful. While Israel longed for Egypt, God longed for a faithful and trusting Israel. God would show them what they were longing for in their desire to return to Egypt – they wanted to depart from the way of deliverance and life and return again to that separated life where devils speaks from the shadows and death becomes destiny. The object lesson involved snakes, which began appearing in the camp. Venomous snakes were slithering and striking at will. These snakes were best described as fiery, for their bite, like most venomous bites, created an immediate burning sensation as poison made its way through its victim's body. This bite meant that Israel was dying.

Death by snake bite is never immediate. Even the most venomous bites will take forty-five minutes to kill a person.

If you were to die from the average venomous snake, it would more likely take four to six hours after the fangs had pulled out, the snake had disappeared, if no aid was provided. No need for your life to flash before your eyes. You would have lots of time to ponder things, plenty of time to wish the bite had never occurred, and plenty of time to wish you had chosen a different path.

Pain and repentance seem to go hand in hand. Israel was in pain. Pain plus death speeds up repentance even more. It is hard not to commiserate with people in pain, and commiseration is automatic when the one in pain is a family member. All of Israel, bitten and unbitten, were feeling the pain of death. Israel connected the dots and repented of their murmuring and desire for Egypt. Moses interceded on Israel's behalf, and God once again provided deliverance.

How deliverance would be accomplished, as was always the case with Israel's Deliverer, could never be predicted. The only thing predicable was that the action taken never looked as though it was sufficient. In Israel's past, door posts were swept over with hyssop branches dipped in blood and deliverance came. In the past, a rock was struck by a staff and help came. Now a bronze snake would be lifted above the dying community and death would cease as the dying gazed in its direction. Who wouldn't look toward the means of salvation when death is so painfully apparent?

In primitive warfare, the winners hung objects on poles as a sign of victory. It was not unusual to behead the kings and commanders of the defeated armies and place those heads on poles that were then raised up for all to see that the enemy had been defeated.

Here the enemy was venomous snakes. Moses was instructed to fashion a snake out of bronze, attach it to a pole and lift it above the stricken camp. The picture, of a lifeless snake hung on a pole, was meant to convey that the enemy had been judged and the threat was now gone. As the bitten community began to gaze upon this judged snake, healing came with that gaze. To look upon this object, judged and lifted up, meant life to them.

Rich and the others, all one hundred billion, felt poisoned. So many scenes were passing before them that left them numb. They saw things as God saw them, for what they really were. Their history had too many wars, too many conflicts, too much hatred, too much oppression, too much un-forgiveness and too much selfishness. There were too many needs ignored, too many hungry unfed, too many naked unclothed, too many sick and imprisoned unvisited and too many strangers left outside. There was a growing consensus, from the best of Adam's children to the worst, that unless mercy was found in this judgment hall, the outcome was obvious.

Out of the books another event came into view. Everything prior to this had been in black and white, but this event was in color. It brought new meaning to high definition. It involved soldiers, politicians, commoners and religious leaders; all gathered around a wooden cross. Scenes of wooden crosses had shown up a thousand times before, and they always leaned hard toward the lake. This event was different. All other events began to orient themselves toward this event, both good and bad. All that had previously either bent toward the throne or toward the lake were now bending toward this cross. Everything found identification with it.

Rich's wretched life bent toward the cross. So many events from Rich's life, which here in this judgment had caused him shame, were now bending toward the cross. He could see it was true for all others as well. All that had bent toward the lake now bent toward the cross. Though crosses always had epitomized suffering this cross radiated healing. And the victim was different. This victim was innocent. This victim was voluntary. As the sins of the world all bent toward this victim and the cross the scene became vicarious. This scene seemed to take a higher place. Eyes were drawn up to view it. Though crosses always had meant death this cross communicated life.

"Another book was opened, which is the book of life."
Rev. 20:12

It was the responsibility of the Jewish religious leaders to keep their fingers on the pulse of the nation's spiritual life. Whenever the spiritual pulse became rapid, their duty was to determine what was causing the excitement or to identify what movement was underway. As Jesus began his ministry, which was marked by validating miracles, word spread quickly. Israel's pulse picked up. The social network went into high gear. The religious leaders were not left in the dark; they had their informants, as well as those who looked to them for a thumbs-up when new ideas and teachings found their way into the nation's life. New ideas and teachings often made their way among the Jews, some wandering in from the outside, others springing up from within.

The most recent buzz was homegrown, and centered around an itinerant preacher from the hill country. His miracles had been observed and, at least initially, were authenticated by reliable sources. Now the religious leaders needed to assess the message and make sure it was in harmony with theirs.

Nicodemus assumed the task and met Jesus one evening. Jesus did his work out in the open, and during the day.

Nicodemus came to Jesus at night so as to avoid the crowds, and hopefully to find opportunity for an uninterrupted discussion where facts could be discovered about this man and his mission. Nicodemus honored Jesus by calling him Rabbi:

> *"Rabbi, we know you are a teacher who has come from God.*
> *For no one could perform the miraculous signs*
> *you are doing if God were not with him."*
> *John 3:2*

Nicodemus and the other leaders and teachers in Israel sensed that a prophet was now amongst them. Moses had instructed Israel to test the prophets. The miraculous signs were affirming, but what was the message? That was at the question on the heart of Nicodemus. Jesus knew why he had come and he cut to the chase with these words:

> *"I tell you the truth, no one can see the kingdom of God*
> *unless he is born again."*
> *John 3: 3*

The Truth came proclaiming truth. The truth was this: the only way the kingdom of God is perceived and received is through rebirth. Nicodemus, in essence, came asking, "Why are you among us? What is your message?"

Jesus made it clear: I am here because "you must be born again."

You were created by God for God. You were created for the kingdom of God. You have become separated from your purpose for existence. You are alienated and I have come to accomplish reconciliation. You must be born again and I have come to make that happen. It is imperative.

Nicodemus, dull as he was, dull as most of us are, asked:

"How can a man be born when he is old? Surely he cannot enter a second time into his mother's womb to be born!"

John 3:4

Jesus explained that rebirth was not a natural phenomenon. Nothing of this natural world could bring it to pass. The watery birth from our mother's womb brings us into contact with this world. To be born of water means we belong to the elements of this world. To be born of the Spirit is to be born of elements from above. To be born of the Spirit brings us into contact with the world above. To be born of water is to be under the care of a benevolent God who causes rain to fall on all. But that birth does not put us under the banner of the kingdom of God. We are aliens, separated from where we are meant to be. We live in a wilderness, among other voices.

Jesus came amongst humanity only to find them shuffling along wearing very heavy shoes with "other voices" stamped on their soles. Humanity lives restricted lives; there is a ball and chain dimension to our existence. Sin is in the world, and clings to humanity like clay mud clings to your shoes. Yet our lives were meant to be light, not burdensome. Jesus used the wind to describe the freedom that was meant to be ours.

> *"The wind blows wherever it pleases. You hear its sound, but you cannot tell where it comes from or where it is going. So it is with everyone born of the Spirit."*
> *John 3:8*

Humanity was living an earthbound existence. They were created for the kingdom of God. They were created to be free, even as the wind is free.

We associate the wind with the heavens for that is where it does it artistry. The wind takes the clouds and spreads them thin and then piles them up thick. The wind positions them so as the sun sets, these ever-changing formations of white against blue become silver lined. Even when the wind passes through a tree and rustles the leaves, we take it as a heavenly event—it feels like a heavenly visitation.

Jesus explained to Nicodemus that humans were created to be like the wind, moving about freely, being influenced by unseen forces yet having an independence that allowed for their potentialities as free moral agents of God. Jesus explained that we all hear the wind, but you cannot tell where it comes from or where it is going, and so it is with everyone born of the Spirit. The kingdom of God is about such freedom.

But Nicodemus and others were not enjoying such freedom. They lived enslaved lives. Freedom's health was not in their veins; sin had poisoned them. Death was present in the camp. Jesus, who is life and truth, came because dying humankind needed his salvation. This salvation would come even as Israel's salvation in the wilderness came. Salvation would be found as the dying looked upon the judgment of sin raised upon a pole. Salvation for the dying camp would come as that which caused the suffering and death was judged and lifted above the camp. Jesus told Nicodemus

> *"Just as Moses lifted up the snake in the desert, so the*
> *Son of Man must be lifted up, that everyone who*
> *believes in him may have eternal life."*
> *John 3:15*

Nicodemus came to Jesus to get answers, and left with a verdict being rendered. Jesus delivered it this way:

> *"This is the verdict: Light has come into the world, but men loved darkness instead of light because their deeds were evil. Everyone who does evil hates the light, and will not come into the light for fear that his deeds will be exposed. But whoever lives by the truth comes into the light, so that it may be plainly seen that what he has done has been done through God."*
> *John 3:19-21*

The Book of Life stood in contrast to the other books. The other books held record of the deeds of humanity. They were books given more to disobedience and separation and death. The Book of Life was about the deeds of one man. Though names were recorded there, names like Teresa and Paul, it was not about their deeds. No one who came to the life that is in Christ has ever been able to separate Christ's life from their life. None have ever found their obedience to surpass his obedience. None have ever claimed their obedience apart from his obedience. None have ever found a basis for their reconciliation to be grounded in anything but his obedience to go to the cross.

The Book of Life was about life coming to a dying world. Jesus had declared himself to be the way, the truth and the life, adding that no one comes to the Father except through him. As Rich and the others, all one hundred billion, stood between the throne and the lake, stood there before the books and the Book of Life, all other ways were gone. Now only truth stood, for false was irretrievable. Now only life existed, for death too was irretrievable.

Humanity had so longed for more scenes that bent toward the throne. The cross was bending toward the throne and the throne was bending toward the cross. Now humanity was seeing the true meaning of the cross. This was where God truly met man. This was where God met man as he truly was. The throne was bending toward the cross. Sin was at the cross. Sin was on the cross. Sin was judged. Humanity was seeing all this before them and above them. Humanity was drawn to this lifted scene. It was as if they were transported back to Christ's early ministry and were present when he said:

> "... Now is the time for judgment on this world; now the prince of this world will be driven out. But I, when I am lifted up from the earth, will draw all men unto myself."
> John 12:30-32

All that had bent toward the lake now seemed judged. The poison seemed to lose it potency. Death seemed to lose its sting and the grave seemed to lose its victory. Another victor stood before humanity.

"For just as through the disobedience of the one man the many were made sinners, so also through the obedience of the one man the many will be made righteous."
Rom. 5:19

This scene touched their sensibilities as none other. This scene touched on their sins, on their poison. Their dying, separation, alienation, disobedience, guilt and hopelessness all seemed wrapped up in something bigger than their collective rebellion. They felt that to gaze upon this scene was to find salvation. They found that Jesus had already identified with them. They were only now affirming what he had already secured.

Humanity was given eyes to see him who came to seek and to save the lost. On this mountain the shroud that enfolds all people was destroyed. On this mountain, the sheet that covers the nations passed away. On this mountain death was swallowed up forever. For Jesus had become obedient to death, even death on a cross.

Death had come through one man, while life came through another

> *"Therefore God exalted him to the highest place and gave him the*
> *name that is above every name, that at the name of*
> *Jesus every knee should bow, in heaven and on*
> *earth and under the earth, and every*
> *tongue confess that*
> *Jesus Christ is Lord, to the glory of God the Father."*
> *Phil. 2:9-11*

Rich and the others, all one hundred billion of them, looked toward the Book of Life, then looked toward the lake of fire, and then looked toward the throne and understood fully:

> *"If anyone's name was not found written in the book of life,*
> *he was thrown into the lake of fire."*
> *Rev. 20:15*

This judgment is where the temporal is separated from the eternal. It is where spirit is freed from flesh. It is where the old order gives way to a new order, where the present gives way to the original. It is where earth gives way to heaven. It is where other voices give way to one voice. It is where all things are renewed.

Rich bent his knee as one hundred billion others' knees bent as well. Rich's tongue offered up in confession what the other one hundred billion tongues were confessing as well—that Jesus Christ is Lord.

14 SHIPTON'S BLINDNESS

Shipton Camp is at 14,000 feet elevation. It is where my oldest son, Matt, and I spent the night before we made our final ascent to the top of Mount Kenya, which is 17,000 feet high. It is far from any significant town or city lights that would pale a night sky. Stars are twice as big in those settings. Black is twice as black. There is a cabin at Shipton Camp that is very basic. The small windows close with wooden shutters. The cabin provides protection from the cold night air and the elements. The night we slept in that cabin was very cloudy. At 14,000 feet we were *in* the sky but the sky could not be seen. No moon, no stars and no light other than the light we brought with us. As our climbing group buried ourselves into our sleeping bags and the last light went out, I became familiar with a darkness I had never known before.

I had watched as the last flashlight went out, and closed my eyes. I had laid there for a while when I heard someone reposition themselves, and I instinctively opened my eyes. There was absolutely no difference visually. I closed them—pitch black, I opened them—pitch black. Open, close, open, close, nothing changed. I thought to myself, so this is what blindness is like.

I have an active imagination. I imagined it was morning, but again when I opened my eyes all I saw was pitch black. I felt the pace of my breathing pick up. I thought, I am so visually oriented I would really struggle if I suddenly suffered blindness. I closed my eyes, I opened my eyes and everything was still pitch black. Then I had one of those stupid moments when a voice inside said, "Maybe you had an altitude reaction and you went blind, high altitude can do that, and people even die at high altitudes. You should consider yourself fortunate that you are only blind."

Another voice countered, "That's ridiculous, I'm not blind—it's just dark in this cabin." The lesser voice said, "If you're not blind, open your eyes and tell me what you see." The better voice said blindly, "I see nothing." This went on for about a minute, until I finally ended the nonsense by feeling around until I found my flashlight and proved once and for all that I was not blind. I often wonder what plan B would have been if my batteries had been dead.

The problem was that I had imagined I was blind. I learned anew that just because we imagine something does not make it true. As I was reaching for my flashlight and some assurance, one hundred parents were tucking their children in and assuring them that just because they imagined a monster in the closet did not mean a monster *was* in the closet. Humbling.

I have spent the last few chapters imagining what the final judgment could be. Obviously it is just that, one person's imagination taking a particular set of convictions and bringing them together with verses from scripture that deal with the final judgment of the human race. I imagine options because I feel the picture painted by the scriptures sets the stage for a final judgment other than what has been passed down.

One thing I have concluded through the years is this: my heavenly Father invites me to connect the dots. He has said things such as, "Consider the lilies of the field," and I connect those dots when it comes to providential sustenance. He has said, "Observe the ant," and I connect those dots in relation to personal responsibility. "Hear the wind" holds a lesson about freedom. My heavenly Father has also said, "Jesus came as Savior of the world," and I connect those dots when it comes to fallen humanity. "Jesus came to destroy the works of Satan" and I connect those dots when it comes to our alienation and reconciliation.

I mentioned early on that I allow for alternative definitions, which in turn allows for alternative arrangements when it comes to the statements I make. I understand and define "eternal punishment" as focusing on the nature of the punishment rather than on its duration. I understand and define Hell is a means to an end and not the end itself. I understand and define predestination as a call to conform to the image of Christ. And I understand and define faith as an activity that is born from above enabling our hearts and ears to hear obediently the better voice.

I have also stated that I have a high view of the work of Christ. I see him as Savior of the world; that is why he came, and that is what he accomplished. And I join many who are convinced we were created to know God and to enjoy him forever. We believe this is true for each of us as well as all of us. And many of us believe God's purpose in this regard will not be thwarted. We eagerly await the day when he will announce from his throne:

"I am making everything new."   *Rev. 21:5*

For it was said long ago:

155

"The perishable must clothe itself with the imperishable, and the mortal with immortality. When the perishable has been clothed with the imperishable, and the mortal with immortality, then the saying that is written will come true: 'Death has been swallowed up in victory.'

"Where, O death, is your victory? Where, O death, is your sting?

"The sting of death is sin, and the power of sin is the law. But thanks be to God!

He gives us the victory through our Lord Jesus Christ."

1 Cor. 15:53-57

And these things must happen, even as you must be born again.

Stand firm.

"See, the storm of the Lord will burst out in wrath, a driving wind swirling down on the heads of the wicked. The fierce anger of the Lord will not turn back until he fully accomplishes the purpose of his heart. In the days to come you will understand this."

Jer. 30:23,24

ACKNOWLEDGMENTS

Others impact our lives without knowing it. When the impact is good we feel obliged to bear witness to those contributions, even when the others have no such expectations.

Many Christian sisters and brothers have openly and honestly expressed dismay with the conclusion of traditional religion regarding the outcome of fallen humanity. That dismay affirmed my desire to write.

I am grateful to authors great and small who have added to my understanding of things.

Deborah Fast has done what I could not: she has brought my writing style in from the playground and forced it to consider other rules and guidelines. I am grateful for her patience and help.

My children are a constant reminder that life needs lived regardless of the task at hand. So I am ever grateful that as they give me space, they also continue to draw me into theirs.

Lastly, I am indebted to my wife who thirty-some years ago agreed to share her life with me. She has the remarkable ability to point to the ground beneath while pointing toward a distant horizon. She has kept me grounded in a forward looking way.

About the author:

Terry Dean McCall completed his undergraduate degree at Philadelphia Biblical University. He then did graduate studies at Columbia International University with an emphasis on missiology. He has also done graduate studies in Germany focusing on international education. McCall and his wife, Amy, have served as missionaries in Haiti, the Dominican Republic and Kenya. In Kenya he served as Chairman of the Bible Department at Rift Valley Academy and taught as Adjunct Professor at Moffat College of Bible in Kijabe. He has also served as an Interim Pastor in a Presbyterian Church in western Pennsylvania as well as a Minister of Discipleship in a Church in Lancaster County where he now lives. He resides in southeastern Pennsylvania with his wife. His children are all nearby. Terry is currently the President of Freedom Climber, LLC, which manufactures and distributes globally his invention, the Freedom Climber.